"A" Teacher, "A" Coach, "A" Man: The Journey to the Heart

Joe Horan

Do you have a story to tell? What's your animal spirit? Share it with us. #hellobeesties

Wildebeest Publishing Company, LLC
6456 Collamer Road
Syracuse, NY 13057

For more information about copyrights and usage, special discounts on bulk purchases, workshops, and engagements, please contact Wildebeest Publishing Company, LLC at (315) 220-0217, info@wildebeestpublishing.com, or online at www.wildebeestpublishing.com

Wildebeest Publishing Company, LLC paperback First Edition April 2023, United States of America

Building Men Creed (written by Coach Mike Masters, founder of Cross Training Athletics) and all other Building Men content is used with permission from Building Men Program, Inc. Building Men Program, Inc. is a charitable organization headquartered in Syracuse, New York www.buildingmenprogram.org

ISBN 978-1-958233-20-7

Dedication

I would like to dedicate this book to my family. The love I continue to receive from my family motivates me to change and grow daily. Without my beautiful wife and children, I would not have learned the hard lessons, been able to see the precious hearts of others, and find the courage to change.

There are so many people God put in my life to encourage, challenge, and walk this journey with me to create an amazing program to help others. Special thank yous to the Building Men family who have supported me throughout the journey to becoming "A" man.

I would like to express great appreciation to my writing team: Tony Tolbert, Heather Marzullo, Jimmy Smith, and Ashley Kang helped create this book. Thanks for pushing me to create a book that, not only, tells a story, but also a journey to manifest change.

Dedication

Table of Contents

Foreword

Fowler High School in 1980 was a special year. At our school, we had a lot of great athletes but could never seem to win a championship. In football, basketball, and many other sports, we were good—but not good enough to bring home a trophy.

Track and field was our last chance to win a team championship. We had a pretty good team that year, one poised to win it all. However, one major obstacle stood in our way: a juggernaut named Christian Brothers Academy (CBA). CBA owned track and field for decades in Syracuse, so most teams were content with simply taking second. Somehow, some way—this year was going to be different.

As expected, Fowler High and CBA swept the conference meets. This created a meet to decide the Syracuse City Schools Champion. The stakes rose when we learned we were competing on their field—where they had not lost in many decades.

As the contest started, the lead changed back and forth. They would win an event and we would win the next!

It boiled down to the last event: the pole vault. CBA had one of the best in our region. Our team's pole vaulter was the author of this book, Joe Horan.

We were deadlocked. Joe was a good pole vaulter. Nowhere near the level of CBA's. They competed intensely and, based on the expectation, it seemed like the CBA pole vaulter would win.

Something happened during the event that changed the trajectory. Joe looked at our team with a look that clearly stated "I won't let you down."

The outcome of the meet came down to the last attempt. The CBA pole vaulter knocked down the bar. Then came Joey (what we called him back then). With a look of determination, he grabbed his pole, ran down the runway, planted, and went up, up, and up!

He cleared the bar; Fowler beat the juggernaut, and we won the championship. Pandemonium on their track ensued.

His eyes then said "I wouldn't let you down," and today via the Building Men's Program-Joe is still saying—"I won't let you down."

Only this time he's saying it to the young men of Syracuse who are at risk, just like he and I were back in the '70s–'80s in Syracuse. The Building Men Program's motto is "Become A man instead of THE man!" By not letting the boys of Syracuse, NY, down in many schools throughout the city school district he is transforming the lives of all young men throughout the city.

This book will become an excellent resource for anyone working with minority or at-risk youth because Joe pours his close to two decades of youth engagement and experience into practical strategies to inspire and transform. His model has been well-worked out and researched over the years.

I have had the chance to work with his students countless times, as a speaker and each time walked away inspired and hopeful for the young men who are currently in similar situations to us, those many years ago.

His passion for helping these young men will have a residual impact on families throughout the city of Syracuse, NY.

Joe is not only a friend, but he is also a colleague in the quest to transform young lives via effective delivery of services coupled with effective relationship-building systems.

Don't just read the book. Study it. Review it with your teams and make it a workable tool. If properly implemented, the suggestions and insights he makes could empower your boys—in the same manner, he and his team inspired theirs.

Enjoy the journey. Learn and grow. This book will be one you may need to read repeatedly, as all good books typically are.

It is again my honor to write this forward and share how I am proud of the work of Joe Horan, his team, and the Building Men Program.

Darrell "Coach D" Andrews

1980 Fowler High School Graduate (SCSD)

Internationally Acclaimed Workforce And Education Consultant/ Speaker

Author:

- *Believing The HYPE-Seven Keys To Motivating Students of Color*
- *The Parent As Coach-Developing A Family Dream Team*
- *The Purpose Living Teen-A Teen's Guide To Living Your Dreams*

Introduction

Looking back 18 years ago...

I was a shell of a man, full of pain. The bottom dropped out of my life after three short years of marriage. All my life I heard "be the best, work hard, and be successful," so I strived to be the best teacher, coach, and husband I could be. I didn't know what I did wrong in my journey of becoming a man, but I do remember standing in the gym with my heart full of empathy like it was yesterday. As I looked around the middle school gym during physical education class, I began to wonder, what could I do to help these boys so they won't experience the same pain I experienced on their path to manhood?

At that time, I was putting up a front or "capping," as the boys say. I chased the image of success that I thought would help me achieve all the stereotypes of a successful man. When my life crashed, I realized that I lacked real substance and depth inside my heart. Instead of striving to be "A" man, I was "The" man, having chased society's definition of manhood. I completely missed becoming the type of man that would have real happiness and fulfillment. Everything I was taught by society's standards to be successful, I strived to reach. I was living what I thought was my destiny; teaching physical education, coaching at the varsity level, being married, living in a big house, and having money in the bank.

During a bitterly cold January, the unthinkable happened. My perfect life, as defined by society, started to crumble. I had reached the varsity coaching level in girls' soccer and softball and found a level of success and comfort teaching physical education. I had gotten married and we planned on having a family. We even purchased a large home with four bedrooms. Life was good.

As I sat by the blazing fire in my perfect yet empty home, I couldn't keep my life together. Unable to be my authentic self, to be "A" man not "The" man, my wife and I separated. I was left hurt and wondering where to go next in life. I would soon realize I was trying to live a myth this whole time, chasing an old narrative of masculinity. I was living my life based on a type of manhood that was not real – one that was founded on a false sense of security driven by money, women, and popularity. Not a version based on values which left me wondering – Where should I go next? Which way is the right way?

I was also asking myself, "How did this happen?" Having worked in schools as a physical education teacher and coach I thought I knew what success in life was about and was accurately conveying it to my students. As a successful educator/mentor, you are taught to meet the students where they are, create relationships inside and outside of school, relate shared experiences, choose empathy, and connect with your students. This is what I believed I was doing daily. As I reflected, I realized I wasn't capable of doing this on a personal or relational level. I questioned what it meant to be a man, a caring teacher, and a loving coach. When I began my teaching career, I wanted to make a positive impact on my students and players. I hoped to make changes to help the community and youth I was working with every day.

In retrospect, I hadn't processed the trauma and hurt in my own life, making it impossible to relate to the hurt and trauma in others. The personal honesty I lacked put me at a disadvantage working with students, so why in my heart was I drawn to work with them? Could I find the healing I so desperately needed and move past the trauma to help these children?

Inspired by the book, *Season of Life: A Football Star, A Boy, A Journey to Manhood by Jeffrey Marx* (2004) I knew that I needed to use the pain I experienced to create a change in my life and the lives of others, particularly the students I taught and coached. First, I had to learn to do the internal work and become an authentic man if I ever wanted to make a real impact working with our youth.

As I started to deal with my pain, my new purpose in life was discovered creating and implementing the Building Men Program. Building Men is a group mentoring program for middle school boys that uses activities, character talks, guest speakers, sports, fitness, and community service to teach the boys how to be "A" man not "The" man. The process of creating this program taught me how to relate to and love students, guide them, and help them become capable of growing up in this society to be "A" man who are real authentic versions of themselves. During the program, we reference sports, current events, life situations, movies, and trending videos to engage them in conversations and talk about real-life issues to help in their development. The goal is to help them see manhood in a new light. Building Men became a way I could learn to love, support, and develop relationships to mentor boys and help them avoid the same pain I had experienced in my life.

This journey of developing and implementing the Building Men Program helps each boy become "A" man in the community by guiding them to think about the different aspects of becoming a man. Not only did Building Men positively impact the boys' lives, but it was a catalyst for change in my life and the lives of a number of staff members. Over the years, it has been like a veil has lifted from my eyes to reveal life lessons, core values, and real love.

This book will describe my journey of change that led to creating and implementing the Building Men Program in the Syracuse City School District. This urban district in Central New York is composed of 31 schools educating over 20,000, where 80% of students are minorities. This book tells the true story of the events that inspired a program and the people with the passion to transform the lives of young boys into authentic men. While designing and implementing this program, my teaching, coaching, and life have been transformed for the better. Finally, the wide-eyed dream of my early teaching days of legitimately helping students was now possible. I was shown a way to make real, lasting change in the lives of young men and their communities.

All the aspects of my life have culminated in the creation of the Building Men Program. This book documents time from my youth to today and my roles as a teacher, coach, husband, father, ally, and an ally/ mentor. In the following stories, I have changed the names of the students and staff to respect their privacy. At the end of chapters three through ten, I summarize key points that have helped me make transformational changes in my life. I share these lessons to encourage, inspire, and motivate others to do the internal work needed to impart meaningful change. It's these changes that helped reshape my heart and can guide others to transformation as well. Finally, as we all need to practice reflection to become the best version of ourselves, thought-provoking questions are provided following each chapter.

CHAPTER I

Society Said
This is Success

AROUND SIX MONTHS after I was separated from my first wife; my sister Debbie bought me a book. I remember being on the phone with her and she said, "My boss said you need to read this book. It's fantastic. You will really enjoy it!" Later that week, I swung over to Barnes and Noble and grabbed the book. I had more time on my hands and was looking for things to keep my mind occupied, so I didn't think about the pain and loss of my ruined marriage. The crazy part was her boss had no idea what was going on inside my heart. He gave her the book *Season of Life,* by Jeffrey Marx; it is about the life of football star Joe Ehrmann. This book turned out to be the catalyst of the Building Men Program.

In the book, Ehrmann talks about the three myths of masculinity. In reading, I began to see how I followed and believed these myths. The first was: to be "the" man you need to be the best athlete. I always dreamed of being a great basketball player for as long as I remember. I would pretend to be in the NBA, on the court as the clock winds down and hitting the game-winning shot. My dad once said I would "marry a basketball one day." Of course, I would be a Boston Celtic, my heroes were JoJo White and John Havlicek. But I never made it to the pros.

On the basketball courts, I remember feeling my manhood status rise on the victories and feeling crushed after the defeats. I was basing my masculinity on the outcomes of those games or any athletic competition I was involved with at the time. There were times that I never felt good enough, especially when I lost and didn't measure up to the athletic abilities of others.

The second myth Ehrmann noticed is that you needed to be successful with the ladies, to be with the best-looking girl or have many girls. I struggled to stay in a lasting relationship. I kept thinking there was a better or prettier girl for me. This myth that happiness could be found in someone else left me with many broken relationships and feeling empty. The women I wanted to have in my life to feel happy always seemed outside my grasp. I am not proud to say, at that time I was more of a user of people than a partner.

The last myth deals with the ability to make money, lots of money. To be the man, you need to make money and be wealthy. My job history was never in the big money industries. I became a physical education teacher and wasn't earning a six-figure salary or on the road to obtaining wealth. I would not say I believed these myths out loud, but in my actions, I showed that they were certainly true in my life.

As I read through the book, I related to Ehrmann's hurt, his despair. I saw the need and felt a desire for change. I started to recognize why there was an emptiness inside my heart. Most of my life, it seemed that other people knew the secret to a happy life, and I felt like I never could reach that level of happiness. It was a strange but comforting feeling to know that I wasn't the only person that lacked the understanding of true happiness.

As I processed this new information, I began to examine the three myths and how they impacted my life. I turned my attention to the boys I taught each day. I remember looking around the gym and saying to myself, "these boys might go through my same pain if I don't teach them a different way." I started asking myself many questions. What is going to prevent them from believing the same myths? Will they be consumed with striving for the pre-prescribed life: marriage, job, house, and money, and miss the true aspects of life? Little did I know, these questions were the early sparks that would ignite my life's purpose. I felt the need to share with them the lessons I was learning while I was building the man I would become. Could I help these young men avoid similar feelings of heartache?

Skiddy Park

In the summer just before I entered fifth grade, we moved from a small house with no basketball court to a huge house, but more importantly to me, it was across the street from a park. When I wasn't in school, I was at Skiddy Park playing sports. The park was one city block, in the middle of the near west side of Syracuse. It contains a softball field definitely big enough to play football and soccer in the grassy outfield. There were two basketball courts, one in front of my house that the majority of the younger kids played on and the one on the other side where the older boys played intense full-court games. In the middle of the park was a lonely tennis court, not many kids played tennis in my neighborhood. Next to the tennis court, was a playground and a clubhouse for staff which had bathrooms that were always locked up. Off to the side of the clubhouse was a sprinkler that was turned on in May and ran all summer to Labor Day.

Skiddy Park was where I fell in love with basketball, which became all I wanted to do. While my family and friends would want to go swimming in the summer, all I wanted to do was play basketball. I can still feel the heat coming up through the bottoms of my Kmart sneakers and smell the sweat ring around my basketball hat worn backwards to keep my long hair out of my eyes when I was shooting. In the winter, I was the crazy kid that shoveled snow off the court just to get some shots up.

To get me in the house while I was playing basketball, my parents would ring the bell. The guys would stop for a second and say, "Joey, time for dinner." Which I would follow up with, "shut up and play ball." It was normal for a neighborhood kid to come to the door anytime during the day to borrow my basketball if I wasn't out there on the court. Almost all the money I made from odd jobs went to buying basketballs. I knew the best place to buy a basketball: the Reliable Jewelry shop on Warren Street downtown. If I could be a great basketball player, I would feel successful.

While the park was a place I found peace and belonging, at times it was a brutal place where bullies and words crushed my hopes and dreams. During an intense game, I was bullied and made fun of by my friends, whether it was my appearance, lack of strength, or athletic ability. I learned very quickly to protect myself. I need to be quick-witted and have a sharp tongue to keep the other kids at bay. While I learned these defense mechanisms of making fun of others' appearances, talking about their mothers, or cussing, this didn't create healthy relationships. I pretended that the comments they made about me didn't have any impact but I took these comments to heart. I started to believe the bullies and would tell myself I wasn't good enough. These insecurities grew over the years. I put up a good front, thinking I wasn't supposed to tell anyone how I was feeling. I was told most of my childhood how lucky I was, having such a great family. I thought I was going to be alright. I never dealt with these childhood feelings or talked with anyone about them.

Smaller Family

Growing up on the lower west side of Syracuse, New York we had an average-sized family for that neighborhood, six siblings! With that many siblings you'd think honest communication would come easily to me, but our focus was on survival and lending service to others. My neighborhood's fame was being cited as top 10 in the country for our poverty rate. We didn't have much financially during those times, but my family always had what we needed. Like other families, we received some government food from the food pantry. There is nothing better than a PB&J sandwich or grilled cheese especially when you use government cheese. The government peanut butter was thick and really sticks to the roof of your mouth. I learned from my mother the numerous and creative food dishes that can be made with beans. My family would receive new clothes when we opened our door in the morning to see a few brown bags on our porch.

One day there were two silky, floral dress shirts that were my size in a brown bag left on my porch. In my sense of style and fashion, these shirts were hip or as the young kids today would say, "fire." I loved these shirts.

My family grew up at St. Lucy's Academy School where I went to school from fifth to eighth grades. We also attended church there; I was an altar boy. Being an altar boy had its perks. I would get out of class when there was a funeral or a special mass and I developed a good relationship with the priest. This was helpful in the winter when my friends and I could get the keys to the gym to play basketball all day. As a family, we attended church regularly throughout my teenage years as I adopted the many Christian values I learned and tried to put into my life at the time. My parents ran a youth group that I attended with my sisters, brothers, and friends in my neighborhood. Even though some days I attended just because of the girls, I found peace and love in the group. It was a place I didn't have to perform or be someone I wasn't. I was accepted for just being myself.

My dad was a deacon in the church for some time. He started working part-time at his job at General Electric and began serving in the church on a regular basis. I learned faith that worked from this experience. Our family's needs were met during this time by others in the church through donations and the church's food pantry. I learned that to serve God, you need to live in poverty and serve others. Our family drove a big green 12-passenger van. When someone in the church needed to move, we took the seats out of the van and became the moving company. When we got a request, dad would have me call a few friends to help. The idea of service became firmly planted in the foundation of our lives as several weekends out of the year were spent moving families.

Junior high

Middle school was the best time ever for me. I experienced some academic and athletic success and made some good friends at St. Lucy's Academy. I was the starting point guard on the basketball team. The classes were good. I did what I was told to: stay out of trouble and play sports. When I wasn't playing basketball, I went to Vincent House for an after-school program. There would be college students who would be our group leaders, and we did various arts and crafts activities, sports, field trips, and there was even a small basketball league.

Vincent House had a camp in the summer in Tully N.Y. only a half hour south of Syracuse on Tully Lake. This is the first time in my life I experienced a love for something other than basketball. This camp was the most amazing experience for me, so much so that I wanted to attend more than one week each summer. This became the only other place besides the basketball court that I felt at home. I loved getting up in the morning, walking to the flagpole, and getting dew all over my sneakers as we stretched in the early morning sun. After announcements and the camp song, we walked to the dining hall following the smell of pancakes, which I covered with too much syrup because my parents weren't there to watch me. All day we participated in activities like canoeing, fishing, swimming, and arts & crafts while making new friends. I dreamed of one day working with all the great counselors that I thought were so cool and awesome.

My favorite game was kick-the-can, a game of speed, stealth, camper intellect, and laughter. Each evening just before dinner the counselor would get an empty #10 can, the one vanilla pudding came in (by the way, there is nothing better than vanilla pudding in a #10 can with vanilla wafers). He'd put one foot on the can and count to 25 slowly. All the campers would hide. The object of the game was to run up and kick the can before the counselor could put a foot back on the can and call out your name. We played this game every day and tried to outwit the counselor. The day would not be complete without camp food like goulash, meatloaf, spaghetti with some type of meat sauce, and dessert followed by an all-camp activity. The day would end by the campfire with the counselor telling the boys in our cabin ghost stories. I looked forward to camp every summer.

St. Lucy's Academy was a kindergarten to eighth grade school at that time, so for ninth grade I attended Blodgett Junior High, located on a diagonal across from Skiddy Park near my house. Compared to St. Lucy's, one classroom of 20 students per grade, the junior high was huge with over 80 students per grade level in seventh through ninth grades. I was prepared to handle the academics but getting used to the large number of students was difficult. Not all the students were from my neighborhood, some were bused in from other neighborhoods more than one mile away. I made new friends with some guys and girls who were in all my classes. This group of us would continue in the same classes at G.W. Fowler High School.

By playing soccer at Skiddy Park and basketball at Vincent House, my athletic career had a jump start at Blodgett Junior High. Calvin, my basketball teammate at Vincent House, picked me for his intramural team. Being selected on Calvin's team helped me get a serious look from the basketball coach, and I made the junior high team at Blodgett. My neighborhood soccer friends, Jose and Mickey, talked me up to their varsity soccer coach helping me make the varsity soccer team at Fowler High School. Sports helped me make friendships, stay out of trouble, and provided a reason to show up to school every day.

High school

I walked to high school every day with my best friend, Howie. He met me at my house every morning as I downed a bowl of Rice Krispies, sometimes with sliced bananas. With a family of seven children, we didn't always get bananas on the cereal, and only on rare occasions was there sugar cereal in the cupboards. Every day we walked seven blocks to G.W. Fowler High School. We always made it on time for homeroom. During my senior year, I had perfect attendance in Homeroom. I can't say I made it to all my classes, having a McDonald's across the street was too tempting! Everyone loves the Egg McMuffin! My high school career was spent running with a small group of friends that were tracked in the same classes year after year.

My academic goals were to keep at least an 85% average so I could play sports and not get grounded by my parents. I never thought my low grades would prevent me from getting into the college I wanted to attend. My teachers and parents would stress the importance of a good education, but I was more concerned with playing sports. I learned to give what they wanted to get what I needed. I would study just enough to earn the grades needed to play. Fortunately, or unfortunately, I was a good test taker, except for the SAT. My SAT score was a 750. My lack of reading in school really hurt me on standardized testing.

I did the usual teenage rebellious stuff with my friends, like stealing fruit from the neighbor's fruit and vegetable truck, sneaking into abandoned buildings, and smoking cigarettes on the railroad track. My dad had the Bulger roll-your-own non-filtered cigarette machine and tobacco. I would roll a few for him because I was a great son. I took a few on the side for myself. I met up with my friend and got sick smoking non-filter cigarettes on the railroad tracks. Smarter teens would start with cigarettes with filters or nowadays vaping, I went right for the hard-core tobacco and paid the price.

Uprooting to a new place

The message I remember hearing growing up was: hard work makes you successful. If you fall, pull yourself up by the bootstraps, brush yourself off, and get to work. All I knew was to work hard to get into college. This was supposed to help me grab the success I wanted and live a happy life. I didn't get accepted to any of the four-year colleges of my choice. But I did get accepted into Herkimer County Community College (HCCC) about an hour east of Syracuse.

I moved into an apartment with three other guys from different parts of central New York. The day I moved in was a party that never stopped. I tried to fit in as well as keep my focus on my education, athletes, and values. It took only two short months before I gave up my values to fit in with my roommates. I stopped living my truth and I started to follow the crowd, looking for acceptance and love from my peers. Slowly over the next few months, I went from an athlete to an 18 year old college student that struggled with an alcohol and drug addiction riddled by fear and guilt. I felt inadequate and insecure in school and among my new friends. Not knowing what to do, I went to the narrative I learned in the city parks and high school. I set out to do what I thought would work: be popular, be the best athlete I could be, and find a girlfriend.

I thought college was a game to be played, not an institution for an education. I went to college because I was supposed to go. It had been the plan from the beginning. The college game was to give the faculty what they wanted, and in return, I'd receive grades high enough to stay in school. I didn't think the family and church values I learned – love, service, faith, moral reasoning – would bring me acceptance in college. By leaving my values, I lost my anchor in life and was sent down a river of destruction I never saw coming.

I entered Herkimer as a radio and television major. I wanted to be a radio DJ. Everything was going well until it was time to sign up for a radio spot. All the radio and television majors met in the large lecture hall to go over the procedure to sign up for your radio time slot. The college radio station was listened to all over campus on the radio. The thought came into my head for the first time, "if I am on the radio, people will listen, what if I make a mistake?" This thought scared me. The more I thought, the fear of what others would think of me grew. I went to my college advisor and asked about changing my major. When asked what my interests were I responded by telling him I like sports but I didn't want to be a gym teacher; I mean a physical education teacher. I thought being an athletic trainer might be cool, I did like being part of a team. I like kids. Maybe I could be a camp director. Camp was always a place I could truly be myself and feel at peace. This resulted in changing majors three times, which landed me as a physical education major. I never imagined being a teacher.

Part of the reason I applied to HCCC was to run track. I heard from my high school track coach that the Herkimer track coach showed some interest in me running for his team. I started running indoor and outdoor track, but the social life in college started to take hold of my life. What started out as going to parties and bars on the weekend, became drinking four days a week, to five. Eventually, I was not at college to get an education.

Over the course of two years, drinking became the most important thing in my life. I dismissed my values in exchange for an addiction. I stopped going to church. I didn't go home because I was ashamed. My college track performance went downhill. I was caught at the bar after curfew the night before a big meet and spent the next morning drinking water and eating carbs to calm my stomach. This didn't work as I let my team down. Feeling ashamed, I isolated myself from my team and stopped trying to develop healthy relationships. I was left with trying to be the life of the party. I longed to feel a sense of belonging. I did not measure up to the other guys at college. I was not able to find my identity in being the best athlete. There were faster and stronger guys on the track team. I was getting beat regularly at different sports in my physical education classes. In the classroom, I was in remedial English and had a hard time excelling in my academic work. I couldn't keep a healthy relationship. Even lost my girlfriend who ended up dating my roommate. Having never dealt with the childhood experiences of being bullied and feeling insecure, I continued to struggle with my sense of worth and belonging. This led to my intense feelings of insecurity which fed my desire to drink and do drugs. When I looked at other guys, I never measured up, didn't feel good enough, so I numbed to forget those imagined inadequacies.

At the end of my first year of college, I returned home for the summer. My family has always been involved with Huntington Family Center, as many of my brothers and sisters attended the center's after-school programming. I heard that there was a camp counselor job available for the summer. Huntington Family Center Camp had a fantastic camp on Bradley Brook Reservoir in West Eaton, New York. I was fortunate enough to work there for the next four summers while I was in college. What I found was magical to me. Camp was a place I could be my authentic self. I felt at home working with kids. The staff and kids accepted me and liked me for myself. I didn't have to put on a mask and try to be someone else. There wasn't any pressure to fit in. No specific fashion code, special skills, and pretense. I didn't have to conform to a preconceived idea of how a camp counselor should act and talk. Camp was where I belonged. I could just be me. I found a place where I felt like I belonged and was accepted. When college ended, I wouldn't find this feeling again for many years.

A new start — same result

After two years and one semester, I transferred to Cortland College. Herkimer and Cortland, both State University of New York schools, had an automatic transfer policy if you had a 2.5 grade point average, which I barely had achieved. I hoped with a new school and environment I could get a new start, get myself under control, and find success. I decided I would try running track again. I renewed my passion for being a camp director, and I hoped that things would be different this time. It didn't take long to find the students that were more interested in partying and less interested in education. I fell into the same destructive patterns.

I spent the next two years at SUNY Cortland living a life of obligation and duty, trying to do what I thought the professors and fellow students expected. I met some great people, had some fun experiences, but I lost touch with my heart. When I was younger I spent nearly everyday with my best friend Harold. We talked about everything. I left the college without a single friendship. I just wanted to be invisible. It was instilled in me as a child to behave. Don't be the one that gets in trouble, causes any additional issues, or says the wrong thing. Don't be seen or heard, keep your head down and follow the rules. I learned not to talk about the issues, just do the right thing and everything will be okay. I knew I was failing, but there was no one to confide in.

During my fourth semester at SUNY Cortland, things got out of control. I was getting high or drinking every day. I tried to participate in sports only to injure my knee during the first game of intramural basketball.

After my first physical therapy appointment, I walked around Cortland aimlessly, lost and alone, with a bottle in my hand. When I did attend class, which was seldom, I was usually under the influence. The only way I knew how to deal with feelings of shame, guilt, and depression was to run away into drugs and alcohol. I dropped out of school to get a handle on my life, nine credit hours short of graduating. I hoped that changing the environment would help me gain control of my life.

Yup, I'm a dropout

I dropped out of college hoping that being back home and finding a job would be the answer. I started working part-time at a local community center in the teen department. I really enjoyed working with the teens, going on field trips around the city in the van, playing different sports, and even doing arts and crafts. I felt a small sense of purpose growing inside my heart as I tried to guide these youth in the right direction. Although this sense of purpose was starting to grow, it didn't fix my personal problems. I continued to struggle with drinking, which led to many selfish decisions, ruining relationships with coworkers and my supervisor. Instead of dealing with the root of the problem, I blamed others for my situation and quit the position.

Next, I started working weekends at Catholic Charities USA youth home for teenage girls. The only reason I got this job was my sister Debbie worked there and put in a good word for me. I worked there for a while to get some money, as well as working at a Mobil Gas station. My drinking was destroying my relationships with the people in my life. I was ashamed of who I became, so I isolated myself from the very people who loved me and wanted the best for my life. There were people along the way that tried to help me: a counselor at college, my parish priest, and a few different church members. These people all had great advice and wisdom, but if you are not completely honest with the people that are trying to help you, you don't get help. It is like going to the doctor's office with a broken arm, telling the doctor that you have a headache, and leaving the doctor's office wondering why your arm doesn't feel better. I never told anyone the whole story. I didn't need anyone else, I could figure this out and get myself together.

Drinking became more important than people, and it started to become more important than my life itself. I ended up depressed, feeling like life was not worth living. I remember being on my knees crying and saying an honest prayer for help. I was going nowhere. I was unemployable and had gotten kicked out of my apartment. I ended up back at home living with my mother, who welcomed me back with open arms. She never judged – just loved me.

At this low point in my life, I was finally willing to believe someone other than myself. My mother suggested I speak to a family friend who attended Al-Anon Family groups. Al-Anon groups help families of alcoholics. I spoke with her and agreed to meet her at a meeting. That short conversation started a journey toward recovery. For the first time, I surrendered to the fact that I didn't have all the answers to life. I became open to receiving guidance from others.

I went to a few meetings and saw a family friend at a meeting. I painted his house as a side job a few years prior. I called him for help, showing up to his office with a list of questions. I took a moral inventory and prepared to take the next steps to get better. He told me to stop blaming everyone else and deal with my drinking. "If you leave now, you can make it to an AA meeting," he advised. There was a sense in my gut that he was right. For the first time in my life, I believed that someone knew how to help me with my drugs and alcohol problem. I can't explain it, but I knew it was the grace of God. I went to an AA meeting, and the only thing I remember was an overwhelming feeling that I belonged. I started seeking help with my struggles with alcohol and drugs. I met many men and women who would be instrumental in changing my life. There was a higher power, God, that had a purpose for my life.

This started my long road to recovery in AA. By going to meetings and learning how to have real conversations, I started talking about my feelings. I would explain to someone how angry I felt and he would tell me that I was hurt. This started the process of identifying my feelings and talking about them with others. It was in AA that I learned about my feelings and that it's healthy to talk about them. I needed healing from experiences which I never talked about with anyone. I had harbored these feelings and experiences in my heart that grew into resentments and unhealthy defects of character that plagued my life. What I really wanted was to shed my shame and guilt. The spiritual aspects of my life I ignored since leaving high school needed to be addressed, not to mention the importance of healing the harm I caused others.

Trying to get my life back

After I stopped drinking and started the journey to sobriety with the help of God and AA, I decided to return to Cortland College and finish my degree in physical education. Reflecting on the experiences that made me feel most content, becoming a physical education teacher made the most sense. I was 24 credit hours and a student teaching placement away from being certified and this seemed like a good option for me. I worked part-time as a waiter at the Glen Loch Mill restaurant and commuted to SUNY Cortland.

After graduating, I had an opportunity to be an assistant camp director at Camp Tousey during the summer. It was a good experience as I had wanted to be a camp director since age 13. As that summer ended, I was blessed with an incredible opportunity. My High School Athletic Director was retiring. One of his final requests was to get me a job. He asked the Syracuse City School District Physical Education department director to offer me a teaching job.

I worked part-time as a teacher in the Syracuse City School District. Additionally, I started coaching at my old high school, G.W. Fowler. I felt like my life was back on track. I got a full-time job teaching in the Syracuse City School district shortly thereafter and started up the ladder of coaching and teaching success.

After several years teaching physical education and working hard at my coaching career, I reached the level of varsity coach, not in one sport but two. I met a school counselor who shared the same love for coaching. She seemed pretty interested in getting to know me and we started dating. Over the course of the next year, the dream of having a family seemed likely. We both loved sports, especially track and field. This was it. The life I wanted, that I believed would make me happy and feel like a man. We attended a pre-marriage retreat, but I failed to answer the hard questions. The doubts in my heart were outweighed by the idea of marriage and being loved. I ignored the feeling that something wasn't right, pushing onward with how I thought life was supposed to be lived.

We got married, and next bought a house. I thought I had it all – success in my job, a big house, and some money in the bank. We traveled during school breaks when it didn't interfere with our coaching duties. We strived to support the students we worked with and developed our athletes into champions.

I excelled at my teaching job, climbing the coaching ladder, having the outer exterior of my life shining and polished for all to see. This is what I knew: work hard and strive to the top of your career. Then, the bottom dropped out.

While I chased my vision of success, I wasn't listening to my heart. The importance of relationships, love, and being the best version of myself was absent. My focus was on self-centered desires. I worked to reach a level of financial success to overcome the inner nagging feeling of never having enough. These emotions I had growing up were never resolved, leading to the end of my first marriage. By following my perceptions of success and placing value on the thoughts of others, I ignored doing the internal work my heart needed. I was lost, confused, and hurt – and I failed again.

I didn't realize that the downward spiral began long before I felt the pain of my failed marriage. My inability to be honest with myself, live my truth, deal with my feelings, and be "A" man, brought me to the point of emptiness. This was a huge blow that brought me to my knees. I never got the "how to be a man" handbook. Did I miss something along the way?

Is there another way?

Based on my life's journey to this point, I wasn't on an ideal trajectory to being "A" Man, I had been lost in being THE man for most of my life. How could I be the best mentor and change the narrative and trajectory for the young minds in my school without having found better tools for my own healing? Can teaching character, completing community service, and being part of a brotherhood create positive change in the lives of these young middle school boys? I needed to find a way to teach these boys that there is another way to become "A" man. The pain of broken relationships and the hurt of separation and divorce planted a desire in my heart to help other young men. The need in my heart to find healing from the unhealthy messages I believed about masculinity provided me with a new passion and purpose to help others learn a healthy way to manhood. This purpose and passion brought the next question to the surface: how do I teach this new way of thinking, this new mindset? There was purpose burning within my heart. I needed to take action to create a change.

I felt an overwhelming need to give all my attention to helping the middle school boys at Levy Middle school. I decided to stop chasing my earlier version of success: being a varsity coach. I was spreading myself too thin with a broad spectrum of responsibilities, so I chose to shift my focus to coaching and mentoring middle school boys.

Fairy tales aren't the only myths

Dealing with the myth of masculinity brings me back to the boys in middle school. Were the boys there hearing and following the same three myths? I could see the boys seeking their value and worth in expensive sneakers and clothing. The best athletes were on top of the popularity charts. Most of these young men would not perform in school to their academic potential, as they didn't want to be seen as "smart." The way the middle school boys would chase, hit, and tease girls to get their attention resembled sexual advances more than love and affection. The girls were viewed as objects to have instead of a person to cherish.

Our trending media sources spend time talking about all the problems boys deal with in our society. The public seems to thrive on the bad messaging for our young men. Spend a day watching TV or scrolling social media, and you will get your fill of sex, drugs, drinking, and violence. It is not enough to tell our boys that there is a problem, we need to provide and emphasize a solution. Missing in our society is when and where we should teach boys about healthy masculinity? Challenging society's views is not enough, pointing out the problem doesn't solve it. We need to teach our young boys the solutions. Our boys are born to lead and become men of courage. Can we provide them opportunities to lead and grow into a man in their school and ultimately in our communities?

Another question arose: How do I teach middle school boys to avoid the painful traps and devices that almost ended my life? I learned that ignoring internal problems by self-medicating doesn't work. It will never fix the problem; it is always still there.

My attention turned to helping boys navigate their way through the middle school years. Can I change the culture and provide healthy messages through my teaching and coaching to help these boys? How do I bring about a change in their attitudes and experiences, so they see themselves as ones of high value, giftedness, and having greatness? I wanted and needed to teach the boys, sooner rather than later, the lessons I had learned that helped change my life; a life based on family values, asking for help, being a leader, and serving others.

I learned a new way of life after my divorce, one of seeking guidance from mentors and elders. Most of my life I was afraid of strong successful men, as I lived with constant feelings of inadequacy. I felt like a little boy in their presence. The desire to help others and find healing for my heart drove me to talk with other men. By having deeper conversations about my struggles and emotions with other men, the narrative in my head started to change. I looked forward to talking to my mentor Gene on an early Saturday morning about my divorce and how to have a healthy relationship. I met with a college professor, Graham, about how to interact and teach Black and Brown boys. I had breakfast with my friend, Mark, to discuss being a father and husband. There was a hunger inside to seek knowledge that was missing earlier in my life.

I started to take a deeper look into my biases and to pursue the internal work to change my heart. I began to understand more about being "A" man, but my knowledge stopped when I tried to understand what it was like being a man of color. I went to my Black and Brown mentors with honest questions. We had conversations about how to teach and help young boys of color. This process of humbling myself, although hard in the beginning, was vital to my growth.

I had learned from Joe Ehrmann, that the first step in truly helping others was having the right heart. I started daily disciplines of reading, reflecting, meditating, and praying. I started being grateful for the little things in life and welcoming the journey of each day. Adding these daily habits provided me with the confidence to be my authentic self and change my mindset. I began using these new gifts for the benefit of others.

There is hope

By looking at my own life, I saw how different experiences provided a spark, created a new desire, or embedded a seed for change. I started asking myself how I could create this same type of experience in the minds and hearts of the young men I taught and coached. I wanted to be a farmer and plant some seeds. I began seeking wisdom from others, reading books, and watching videos to find insight into these questions. Was it possible to develop and provide experiences to allow the young men to see the world around them in a different light? Can we challenge society's narrative and concept of manhood? Could teaching the importance of significance, integrity, and relationships help our young men develop a heart for others? This started a journey in which the boys and I would walk together.

I began reading books on manhood and rites of passage. I attended more conferences with the sole purpose of finding a way to transform the hearts of boys. I would get email suggestions for books, movies, videos, and articles to read from colleagues.

The journey entailed finding creative ways to provide boys with different opportunities to open their minds and touch their hearts. Finding opportunities that could provide exposure or perspective and create building blocks to further develop growth.

My path to help the boys in their journey to manhood has brought a healing of my heart, changed my perceptions on life, and given me a new passion and purpose. I soon realized that "building" is a verb, an action. It's not a journey that was read in a book, but rather an adventure to be experienced. In the following chapters, I will share the transformational adventure I took to reach the hearts of the boys, colleagues, and community, through implementation of the Building Men Program.

CHAPTER 2

Lesson Learned in Formative Years

BACK IN THE day, different experiences during my school-aged years shaped how I responded to current situations, good or bad, in my life. These experiences influenced the decisions, choices, and emotions of future experiences. In doing the internal work, I realized these early experiences had a major impact on my teaching, coaching, and working with the Building Men Program. I never fully reflected on and processed the experiences that happened in my early years. Any emotions or hurts were left unhealed in my heart. I have found out that I needed these heart issues to be brought to the light to become a more effective teacher, coach, and "A" man.

Next, I'll share some of the major experiences that have impacted my journey. As a mentor of mine, Boston Frank, would say, "I remember the things that have impacted me. It's good for me to remember these things."

Orange reading group

When I was in fifth grade, my family moved to the west side from the south side of Syracuse, and I attended St. Lucy's Academy. This was where my relationship with books and reading was shaped. The fifth grade classroom was big with a ten-foot ceiling and huge windows in the front of the building. This was great during warm weather, terrible in the winter, drafty and cold. The classroom lacked any home touches, no carpets or furniture like you see nowadays. The best part was the huge coat closet in which I had my first kiss.

My class was small with 18 students and rotating teachers. We went through eight teachers that year. I am not sure the reason why, although I wasn't known for my stellar behavior as a student. In the beginning of the year, to assess our reading skills, we took the SRA test, a standardized test, to help the teachers place students in homogeneous reading groups for instruction. I didn't completely understand the purpose of reading groups at the time, nor the impact of this test.

After the test results were in, the reading class changed, and I changed as well. The teacher would give reading materials to us at our desks and call us to the back of the room by colors. The blue, red, yellow, and green students went to the back first to get their reading work. As it turned out, I was placed in the orange reading group. All five of us in this group knew orange was the worst; we were the poor readers. I hated being called to the reading table last. Sitting on those small, hard plastic chairs doing remedial work made me feel stupid. In the front of the class, my classmates seemed to be having a better time. Their reading lessons seemed to be filled with fun, and when they were finished with their lesson they had choice time. While I was still learning reading, they got to pick their own activities. I wished I could be in the blue or red group, but we remained in these groups for the rest of the year.

From that time to my junior year in high school, I read one book, *All in the Game*, for pleasure that was over one hundred pages in length. All through high school, my reading was limited to the sports page, comics, and required schoolwork. My negative mindset towards reading caused not only a struggle in English class, but in every class. Reading is the fundamental building block of all education, even in math you need to read the word problems. I had a whopping score of 350 on the English part of the SAT, which impacted my ability to be accepted into a four-year college.

The essay

In eighth grade I had the hardest, most demanding teacher in Mr. Levenston. He taught English and social studies at St. Lucy's Academy. Mr. Levenston was the first male teacher, outside of the physical education teacher, I had in my educational career. He assigned an essay every day for homework. Some days he gave us topics for the essay, and other days, we could write about whatever we liked. We needed to have the correct heading and number of written lines before he would accept the essay. If we didn't turn it in, we stayed in class during lunch to make up the homework assignment.

He had a huge impact on me. He was not a yeller, never seemed to enter a power struggle, and was fair yet demanding. An example of this was in the spring semester in social studies, we had to handwrite a 25-page research paper on World War II. Looking back, I needed a strong male presence in my life. I did not like the accountability, but he helped me learn how to be a good student. Of all the other teachers I had, I responded to him differently. I would mess around in his class as my way of dealing with my low abilities, but he always got my attention. I could sense his love and concern for me to succeed. He kept me accountable. I often spent lunch with him to make up for any missing essays. He would talk about the importance of education and my future. When I fell behind, he called home to speak with my parents. I didn't like him at the time for this, but it was what I needed. He really wanted us to learn, and he taught with passion and love. I succeeded with his strong, male presence in my educational life.

Algebra

My eighth-grade math teacher was Sister Theresa. She helped me gain confidence in math, and she regularly told me that I was smart. She helped me believe that I could figure things out, instilled in me a positive attitude towards learning, and taught me to never give up, even when I was struggling. One day she told me, "You are doing in eighth grade what ninth graders are doing in algebra." Sister Theresa worked with me, nurtured me, and helped me believe in my abilities. I continued to junior high with a new confidence. Algebra seemed easier for me than everybody else. Was it actually easier or was it the confidence she instilled in me that helped me succeed?

Lime green suit

For ninth grade, I attended Blodgett Junior High, in the Syracuse City School District. This was a transition from a small Catholic school to a much larger public one. I enjoyed being part of a larger school with a more diverse community. My experience with the teachers, students, and sports there was excellent.

At the end of the school year, my basketball coach told me I was going to get an award at the school ceremony. I was so excited. I didn't know why I was getting the award. I played basketball for the junior high team, but spent most of the game time on the bench. I went home. I got out my best and only suit, which was a hand-me-down.

I got dressed up to receive my award. I slipped on my pair of purple Prokeds and my lime green polyester suit with a brown and yellow flower print shirt. I walked down the street to Blodgett Junior High that evening with this feeling of looking good and ready for the awards ceremony.

I remember going on the stage to receive the award with my good friend Dwayne. Dwayne and I didn't play many games, but we both worked hard every day in practice. The coaches recognized our effort and honored us with a plaque. The award was great, and I took pride in working hard. Still, that was not the big takeaway that night.

I remember hearing people laugh when I walked on stage. As I looked around, I saw how other people were dressed, and I realized that I looked different. I didn't have the same style of clothes the others wore. There was an intense feeling of not fitting in and not measuring up that started to develop. As I walked home, I was more embarrassed than happy. I realized I didn't have the same things as others. This started a shift in me to place greater value on the opinions of others over what was important to me.

Looking back, this subtle shift began a journey away from my core values of faith, love, and worth, leading instead to heartache and pain.

Newspaper reporter

After eighth grade, most teachers did not have an impact on my education or character. By the time I entered 10th grade at G.W. Fowler High School, I learned to play the education game – you gave the teacher what they wanted, and they would give you a good grade. I heard somewhere that I needed grades higher than 80% to get into college. I set my goal to get an 85 average; that's what I thought would be enough to get me into college and play sports. The academic benchmark was to be average, just enough to get by.

In 11th grade English class, I was given a different experience that would touch my heart and plant a seed that would sprout and continue to grow in college. Mrs. Miles was a different type of English teacher. While I still struggled with English and reading, she made a difference. In the third marking period, we were given a class project. Mrs. Miles decided we would create a school newspaper that would be printed and distributed to the entire student body. I was assigned to be one of the sports reporters. This connected my passion for sports to education. My job was to attend games, interview coaches and players, and write articles about high school sports teams. When the newspaper was printed, I saw my articles, my written work, all over the school. I saw that education had meaning and was relevant to my life. Even though I had struggled in English class in earlier grades, she connected my passion with education which sparked a desire to read and write. I read my first novel for pleasure and started writing small projects after this experience as a reporter. This changed my outlook and had a lasting impact.

Physical Education teachers are cool

The first physical education teacher I can remember was at St. Lucy's Academy, Mr. Phillips. He was also the basketball coach when I was in seventh and eighth grades. He seemed like the coolest guy ever. He was fun and inspired me to excel in physical education and sports. We needed to go across the street to the gym for physical education class, even in the winter months, which I never minded. Mr. Phillips would let us stay across the street for a little extra time some days. His classes were active, challenging, and he had a great sense of humor.

Mr. Phillips was the kind of coach that really believed in his team, and you could sense from the way he spoke that he cared and loved us. In seventh grade, he made me feel like part of the team, even though I didn't play that much. He valued all his players the same. He made me one of the captains when I was in eighth grade. Even when I was struggling, he never raised his voice or took me out of the game. We were so happy the day we beat the cross-town rival, St. John the Baptist. Being on his team was a great experience.

My ninth-grade physical education teacher, Mr. Grey, was really into fitness and taught us how to keep our bodies in shape. We played traditional sports, but the magic was the storage room, which he turned into a weight room. It seemed like everyone wanted to take their turn in the weight room. He didn't have a large budget, like most city school teachers, so he used his own resources. He made barbells by taking metal bars and cementing #10 tin cans on the ends, he made dumbbells with broom sticks and plastic milk containers. Nothing could stop him from sharing his passion for fitness with us.

When I attended G.W. Fowler High School, there was a group of young physical education teachers that were awesome to be around. Nowadays in physical education class, I would not be able to do all the activities and stunts in class that they had us doing at that time in high school. We had a huge trampoline set up during class to play Follow the Leader, always trying to outdo each other. We played floor hockey that ended up in a fake brawl in the goal mouth. They let some of the athletes come down eighth period for an extra physical education class so we would stay out of trouble at the end of the day. The physical education department was made up of many of the high school coaches (my soccer coach, a wrestling coach, a baseball coach, and my track coach) that had some of the biggest impacts on my life during my high school years. I think their love, impact, and energy planted the desire in me to teach physical education. This desire didn't come to the surface for many years.

Vincent House camp

My fondest memory growing up was attending sleep-over camp each summer. Well, that was after the first experience which lasted five hours as I needed to be picked up due to homesickness.

I went to Vincent House Camp every year from ages nine to fourteen. There was a dining hall with a long porch that overlooked the water, a boathouse, arts and crafts shack, and six cabins for the campers to sleep. There was a large cabin that served as the summer home for the extra staff and kitchen help. The camp lasted a week – you arrived on Monday and went home Friday after lunch. It was only a few miles away from home, but it seemed like time stood still in this whole new world.

Camp Director Peter was a loving, dynamic, and amazing man who touched my heart. He shared his love for the campers by making a safe and nurturing environment. I looked forward to going to camp all year; I couldn't wait for the magic I would find there. Camp gave me a chance to be me, follow my interests, and make some new friends. To me, camp will always be a safe place to grow, have fun, and be my authentic self.

At 13, when I was too old to be a camper, Peter let me wash dishes for the whole summer. I stayed in a separate cabin with other staff, which was cool for a new teenager. All week, my job was to clean the kitchen and dining room, and wash dishes. When I wasn't cleaning or doing dishes, I could join in on the camp activities with the campers. The director paid my father 50 pounds of sugar for my services that summer, pretty sweet of him. The pay didn't matter to me, because at that time there was something special that I was experiencing in my heart. Being at camp, and part of the staff, sparked a purpose in me. I now knew I wanted to be a camp director. I wanted to be a camp director and create a special place which could impact the lives of other children.

Lost my love — basketball

The love of basketball started at a fourth-grade basketball game at St. Anthony's. I remember all the boys in the two fourth-grade classes were split into teams, and we wore different, colored T-shirts. On the big day, we played basketball after school in the gym. After the game, all I wanted to do was play basketball on my neighbor's basketball hoop. The hoop and backboard were nailed to a tree in their backyard below the treehouse. My neighbor wanted to play army and hang out in the treehouse and only played basketball occasionally. I always wanted to play basketball with the older boys that lived behind my house, but they wanted to play with their older friends. I dreamed of playing basketball with the big guys.

In fifth grade, my wishes were granted, and we moved to the west side of Syracuse right across the street from the courts at Skiddy Park. I was in heaven. I literally walked across the street to the basketball court. I would wake up early when I wasn't in school and beat everyone to the court to shoot and practice new moves. I would stay there all day. There were many times I'd have to bring over the broom to sweep glass off the court, grab some water for everyone, or a quick bite to eat. It was a dream come true. You might remember, I said I was the crazy kid that shoveled snow off the courts to shoot hoops in the winter. I would rather play basketball than read, swim, or any other activity. Sometimes all the guys would want to play soccer, football, or baseball, so I went and played, always hoping they'd pick basketball when we were done.

I was fortunate enough to make the school basketball teams from seventh through tenth grade. I dreamed of being a professional basketball player, a member of the Boston Celtics, but the reality of the situation set in during 11th grade. As a high school junior, I was skinny and short, 150 pounds and 5'8," not your typical high school basketball size. I had an awful tryout where I lost the ball three times as point guard and twisted my ankle. The tryout was summed up when the coach didn't have any ice, so he told me to go stick my foot in the toilet, using its cold water to keep the swelling down. I was cut from varsity basketball. This crushed my heart and spirit for months until I found my way to another sport and a track coach that valued my abilities.

After being let go from basketball, I felt like I lost my love, my identity. At this stage in my life, basketball was my definition of manhood. When I won, I felt like a man. When I lost, I was less of a man. I was convinced of the first myth of masculinity, but I didn't see it at that time. I saw my value in what I did, playing basketball, not on who I was as a person. I felt I couldn't move on from being cut.

Teen Seminar

Another experience that helped mold me was participating in the youth group called Teen Seminar. There wasn't a youth group at my church, but there was a movement among some of the surrounding churches in the Central New York area. Seeing the need in our neighborhood, my parents started a Teen Seminar group. Why not? They had a group of teenagers themselves.

We had a large extra room attached to the back of our house where we met on Mondays to talk about teen issues, relationships, God, spirituality, and struggles we might have been having at the time. This was the safe space where our friends got together to talk, learn, and share how we were dealing with life.

In Teen Seminar, I found the sense of belonging I was searching for, especially after being cut from basketball. This special group of friends was the place I felt like my authentic self. A community of family and friends in which I felt accepted. I still wonder why I stopped looking for a similar community when I went to college.

My Lessons

The formative years of my journey shaped my future in both positive and negative ways. I believe it is important to find out how my past experiences influenced my work and personal life. Below are some lessons I've come to understand through self-assessment.

- Perceiving a stigma as a poor reader can limit motivation in school
- Increased rigor can grow accountability
- Instilling confidence in a student can be a game changer
- Inner narrative of poverty impacts life choices
- Connect education to the student's passion, this will help them learn
- Identity found in sports is fragile, especially when I was cut from my favorite sport
- Belonging provides emotional growth and support

Your Turn:

- How did your early years impact your role as a teacher, coach or youth worker?
- How did your childhood shape your view of being a man?
- In what ways did the experiences in your youth determine the path of life you have chosen?
- Did your upbringing teach you any stereotypes of masculinity?
- Are there personal habits or choices you currently make due to unhealed childhood experiences?

CHAPTER 3

Impactful Choices

AFTER GRADUATING HIGH school, I began making poor decisions. I stopped relying on other mentors and family for advice and direction because I knew what I needed to be to become my own man. I lost the values that were instilled in me during my childhood. I chose to gain acceptance and follow the crowd. I was not equipped to be away from my family and community, as I started to chase the values that society portrays as a successful man.

Through this time of pain and struggle, there were lessons that I learned. Reflecting on these experiences, I have learned lessons of overcoming obstacles, finding mentors, and living by core values. Not only did I learn what was not important for a successful life, but I learned some answers to some hard questions that could help the next person.

Through the trials, I can offer some hope that there is a better way, a way of peace and significance. It's these struggles that shaped my teaching and coaching, and created the Building Men Program. It's through these hard times that I know I can make a difference, and nothing can stop me from touching the hearts of the youth.

It's expected to go to college

I was supposed to go to college, even after I knew I wasn't going to play college basketball. I was brought up hearing my family and their friends talk about the importance of going to college. My parents encouraged us to go. My older sister, Debbie, went to college the year before me. I was to go to a college after high school. Deep down, I was unsure about the whole thing. There was nothing wrong with going to college, but I didn't fully realize what I was supposed to do when I got there. I didn't understand the real goal of attending an institution of higher education. Looking back, I was not mature enough, mentally or emotionally, to be away from my family and community.

This was where I fell into the dominant story of society as a white male. I didn't realize the truth surrounding my downfall until years later. The three myths of masculinity and the dominant male narrative of our culture impacted my behaviors, values, and attitudes. I left my home and tried to fit in with the popular crowd at the expense of life and future.

I am not casting blame. I realized I made decisions to fit in based on what I thought would bring me happiness. I started losing myself and my values.

I did just enough work to pass my classes so I could remain in college to party. I looked for my coaches to help me financially with a part-time job. I ended up using the extra money to cover my drinking habit. The girls I met, I used to boost my masculinity. These relationships were not a two-way street. I had nothing worth giving.

I didn't invest the time to gain the knowledge, experience the opportunities or create a network to become a physical education teacher. At college, the assistant track and field coach tried to help my situation. He shared with me his story and told me I had potential. He advised me that my drinking was holding me back from my true abilities, but I valued the partying life over his guidance. I dismissed the help.

Lost control

After graduating from Herkimer County Community College, I got accepted into State University of New York at Cortland, as there was an automatic acceptance with a 2.5 GPA. I had a chance for a brand new start. Unfortunately, it didn't take long before the same patterns of drinking and drugging began, and I lost the desire to do anything else. After a sad two week attempt at running track at SUNY Cortland, I quit. All my attempts at trying to stop drinking and become a good student and athlete ended at the bar. As you know, my choice to drink/party ultimately set me on a path to AA and paved the road for my growth/internal work, but at the time it derailed the goals I wasn't sure I wanted to make. I could not stop; I could not get out of my own way. I saw a counselor who suggested that I limit myself to two drinks a night. I failed every time. I no longer wanted to go to school. I lost all passion or purpose for my life. The goal of graduating from school went out the window. I ended up dropping out of college nine credit hours short of a degree.

I returned home to live with my mother and get a job. The change of environment didn't fix the problem. I continued to drink for the next couple of years. I tried to be strong and tough to get myself together. I wouldn't ask for help or show any weakness. I ended up jumping from part-time job to part-time job. Living off my family to stay afloat at times, I was caught up in a downward spiral. I tried to fix my life through self-help books. Something was missing in my life; it would be two more years before I would start to see the answers.

Relationships were selfish

It saddens me to admit the number of people, especially women, that I hurt during my college years. I realized that most of my relationships in college were one-sided. I used people for my own selfish reasons. I was incapable of having a real relationship based on love and trust. I was just trying to meet my selfish needs. Looking back, there were some amazing people that tried to establish healthy relationships with me, the type of friends you make for a lifetime, but I was incapable. I missed the concept of being a man, as Joe Ehrmann explained, "having the capacity to love and be loved." I had the "all about me" or "the world revolves around me" mentality. When you are the center of the world, it's a lonely place.

A job at the local community center

After I dropped out of college, I tried to get my life together, find a job, and move forward. I ended up finding a part-time position in the teen department at a local community center. In the teen department was a cozy living room area with couches and loveseat. There was a small kitchen that allowed us to cook often. It was here that we would be teaching life skills to the teens, the same skills I desperately needed to learn. I enjoyed hanging out in the evenings at the teen drop-in center and being a chaperone on field trips. There would be various speakers that would come in to talk with the teens about topics like getting a job, staying away from drugs, and teenage pregnancy.

Living in the neighborhood with these teens, I would see them often and start playing basketball with them at the park. I didn't realize it at the time, but I found my purpose – working with these teenage boys. The big problem was I didn't have knowledge or mentoring skills, so I played a lot of sports with them and tried to be their friend. These boys didn't need me as a friend as much as they needed a mentor to teach them strategies to find success on their own life journey.

The other experience at the teen center which changed the course of my life was when I fell in love with my co-worker. She was the most amazing woman I had ever encountered in my life at that time. We spent everyday together working with the teens, chaperoning field trips, picnics, or just hanging out talking. We started to grow close. She took me to her church as I tried to get my life together. This was hard as I was still drinking. I ended up falling in love with her over the course of a couple of years, but it wasn't the right time for our love. The result of our love was the most precious daughter. Knowing that the timing wasn't right, I quit my job so she could keep working and provide for our daughter.

I continued to struggle with alcohol. I would try to stop drinking only to start again a few weeks later. I would binge drink until I couldn't stand living in my own skin and then stop drinking. I would stay sober as long as I could, but the inner turmoil would be too great. As I sought relief, I would drink again. I was in a cycle I couldn't stop.

Out of respect for her wishes, I separated myself from her and our daughter. This pain and hurt brought me face to face with my addiction. I wouldn't seek help. I moved on with the agreement that when my daughter wanted to see me, I'd be willing. I would need to patiently wait for a miracle to be an active part of her life again.

Wandering, no destination

I just started wandering aimlessly through life, that was the best way I can describe this time period. I didn't have a job, nor motivation to get one. So, I tried to be a salesman for my dad's computer business. I was the child in the family that knew the least about computers, so this didn't pan out too well. Mostly, I sat around feeling sorry for myself and wondering how I got into this position in life. My shame became too great, and I stopped working for my dad. This started a period of time being unemployed. I couldn't afford my apartment and moved in with a family friend who asked me to leave after two months. On the verge of being homeless, my mother took me back in. I was trying to fix myself by reading self-help books and going to different churches, but this didn't work. I could not fix myself, I needed divine help.

I remember one spring day in May being in the living room and not wanting to live anymore, but I couldn't bear the thought of killing myself. I had hit my bottom. I said the first honest, humble prayer in my life and asked God for help. At this point, I was graced with a series of divine experiences that put me in contact with people that would help me, and I finally got to AA. This started my journey of a life of sobriety.

Back to college

The following fall, I returned to college to finish my degree. Being sober and trying to live a different way of life, I reentered college with a different attitude. I was seeking education this time around and I had a ton to learn and relearn.

I went to college for an education, not the social experience. I wanted to be a physical education teacher, coach, and to work with children. My study habits needed to change desperately. I started to do what the college professors and high school teachers had told me to do from the start, sit in the front of the class, participate in discussions, study for tests, and put forth an effort to learn. Going back to school seemed harder, because I was in higher level courses without having learned the expected prior knowledge. This put me at a disadvantage. I needed to relearn what I missed the first three years, as well as learn the new content.

I decided that teaching physical education would be a good career choice for me. I liked working with kids and loved sports. It was like a light switch was turned on. I returned to school for a purpose, my future career. I had a reason to show up every day and put in the time and effort.

Get a job and get married

At this time, I thought my life was going according to the right plan. Success for "the" man meant: get a job, find a wife, buy a house, and have a family. I tried to reach for the dream and obtain some success. What really happened was some hard lessons on humility, selfishness, and pride. As with most lessons in my life, I learned the hard way.

I found some success teaching middle school physical education. Some principals wanted me to move to their buildings. Then different school leaders wanted me to go into administration. I didn't take a different physical education job or get into administration because I found a love for coaching. I moved up the coaching ladder and coached two varsity girls' sports – soccer and softball. I started to gain some notoriety in the coaching community.

My first wife worked in the guidance office. Once we started talking we found out we had many things in common as we both were former track athletes, loved working out, and were passionate about college and high school athletics. Of course, we ended up getting married. She got a job as a guidance counselor in a neighboring district and started coaching sports as well. Without listening to the people in my inner circle, I was excited about my chance to get married, buy a house, and have a family. As we all know, hindsight is 20/20. Looking back, our marriage was based more on my individual wants instead of shared hopes, desires, and wishes.

We followed my plan for success, got married, traveled, and purchased a big house. We continued to work and coach in different school districts. I thought I understood what it meant to be a husband, but I fell dreadfully short. As a couple, I struggled through the veil of pride; I didn't see how bad my relationship was at the time. I didn't want to see the truth about our relationship. Our inability to have children put stress on our marriage. I was not the emotionally supportive husband my wife needed at that time, which put our initial years of marriage in jeopardy. We ended up getting a divorce.

My chase for success and happiness failed. I questioned the purpose for my life. I learned lessons through this experience, some of which were: asking for help, the importance of speaking my truth, being supportive and vulnerable, and humility. I learned that these traits are important in all relationships. Authentic relationships were the key piece missing in my life. Relationships take work, get messy, and, at times, aren't easy. I was faced with the hard questions and I realized I did not have the answers.

A chance at a family

After the divorce, I thought my chances of having my own family with children was washed up. Being a bit older (40), I had already lost an opportunity to bring up my daughter. This hit my heart hard. I decided I couldn't let this situation stop me from having a family. After talking to my mentor, I sought out some professional counseling help to help me solve my relationship problems. This time I listened and put into practice the professional help I received.

There were so many different lies I told myself; I didn't know my truth. I needed help to be able to do the internal work, the work of the heart, to differentiate between the lies and my truth. I started to address these problems through the help of a counselor. Through this work, we found many problems in my past relationships that impacted all other relationships in my life. These problems had to be unpacked and brought to the surface to be dealt with properly. This wise counselor gave me work to do that included things to reflect upon, books to read, journaling, time alone to meditate, and new habits to develop. My mentor helped me develop accountability to finish the process I started. I began to look at all the mistakes in my past relationships. This process put me on a better footing to developing healthy relationships.

One takeaway from these experiences was that relationships are fluid. Relationships don't develop to a certain level and remain there constantly. There is always work to do, like with a garden. To thrive, one must pull weeds, mulch, fertilize, and prune. Now I know the importance of working to establish relationships, and that I must continue to water and nurture them to keep growing.

My Lessons

The impactful choices are the decisions I made, good and bad, in my life's journey which have shaped my teaching, coaching, personal life, and the Building Men Program in different ways. It was through unpacking the lessons, trauma, and results of my choices that enabled me to heal and restore my heart. In the restoration of my heart I can teach, coach, and love others in my life. Things I learned, both positive and negative:

- Seeking approval of others through alcohol and drugs led to addiction and disaster
- Using people for personal gain leads to loneliness
- Education is important and vital to succeed
- Seeking society's "definition" of success is shallow and empty
- Living without values leads down a wrong road

Your Turn:

Think back on your life and reflect on some of those defining moments.

- What shapes the way you view the world?
- Who shapes the way you view others?
- How do you define yourself?
- What is one theme you would give to your life?
- What choices have you made that developed this theme?

CHAPTER 4

A Teacher

I ENTERED THE teaching and coaching profession to make a difference, to help young people grow and develop. I have come to believe in the saying it takes a village to raise a child.

The way our society is set up, teachers can play a positive or negative role in the lives of children. Teachers can teach the curriculum and pick up their paychecks. Some teachers use classroom instruction as a stepping stone to follow their own career aspirations. A number of teachers love their students and teach to their heart by providing them the support and care to become their best selves. Other teachers provide the resources and experiences for their students to succeed. Unfortunately, as a beginner teacher, I believe I missed the mark.

I have watched countless new teachers come into the educational system ready to take on the world only to feel defeated by the system a few years later. New teachers soon become cynical of their abilities to help as they are being pushed to prioritize increasing test scores. These young educators lose their heart and passion for teaching, especially in the urban setting and often end up leaving the profession.

The beginning of my teaching career was about my success and goals. For my success, I needed my students to help me look good during administration observations. My classes needed to be under control and reach my objectives. For my approval, I always wanted someone to look in and see a well-run class. I learned through experience that I can have an impact on the students I teach.

During my early days, I had feelings of defeat. My teaching became de-tached from my heart, and I lost any passion for helping youth. I would only strive to be a good teacher, one that was in control of his class: it was all about me. I started going through the motions of writing lesson plans. I would get mad when a student acted out and disrupted my lesson. I learned to use the classroom management techniques to have power and control of students. I didn't discipline the student with love, the discipline was out of frustration and anger that the student would not follow the directions. I sat them out without a conversation. I failed to restore him back into class. Just sit out and be quiet.

My passion started to wane. Teaching started to become a job, just what I did for a paycheck. Disconnected from my heart, my relationships were all about power and control. I needed to be the best no matter the expense. These characteristics had me roll along and teach for my pride. Although there were many models of excellence when it comes to teaching with passion, there was a larger number of teachers and coaches I watched who discouraged my hopes of making any real changes in youth and in my chosen career path. I fell into the trap of education without a heart.

Start as a teacher assistant
I started at Levy Middle School as a teacher assistant, which at first I did not appreciate. At that time, I was all about judging and being the best, I didn't realize the importance of love and caring for the students.

Years later, I now realize I was blessed with an opportunity to work in an autistic classroom with loving teachers and staff. I watched how to teach students with disabilities from some amazing teachers and teacher assistants who saw the disabled community as amazing, loving people. Many of these students lacked the ability to express themselves verbally. It is like their emotions were caged up; they were not able to express feelings. Some students would hit, pinch or yell as they tried to share their feelings. Other times, they would laugh and dance to communicate their joy. The staff helped me identify their different types of communication, and I started to see these students as children who experience the same hurt, happiness, joy, and sadness as other children. They just couldn't express it verbally.

At first, my ignorance didn't let me see that they had the capacity to communicate, to show love and affection, as well as hurt and pain. These loving students were one of the pathways that taught me I needed the ability to share my heart with all of my students.

What impacted my early years of teaching was being a teaching assistant and being able to observe other teachers. I watched how they loved and respected their students. They were showing me what I needed to learn to be an effective teacher. They taught me the love and respect children needed to learn and grow.

Physical Education

I had been teaching physical education for around 12 years when I attended my first workshop presented by Joe Ehrmann. After this experience, I started reflecting on my performance as a teacher, coach, and staff member in the schools I had worked at during the beginning of my career. I began doing the inside work I needed to accomplish to connect with my heart. How did I, if at all, impact the hearts of the students I taught and coached? It was difficult to look at all the mistakes and lost opportunities during the beginning of my teaching and coaching career.

Looking back, I realized when I started teaching physical education and coaching, my interactions with the boys were with my unhealed heart. In these early days, I brought knowledge, pedagogy, and lesson plans, but never did I bring my heart.

I had work to do as it relates to being a man and healing my heart. The number one myth, the need to be the best athlete, was still very present within. I looked at these male students through the lens of the myth; I judged the best student as needing to be the strongest, biggest, and best athlete. It was years before I self-reflected and saw the damage that this way of thinking had on my students. Instead of nurturing these boys, I was judging them. My inability to deal with my own manhood as well as my lack of knowledge for how to lead with compassion, hurt my students. This had to change to make a difference in their lives.

Power struggles

In the beginning of my career, managing a class was based on power and control. It was my way, and I knew best. While this way of teaching might have produced a well-managed class, it didn't create an environment of caring and creativity. Every time I walked into a classroom with this attitude, I LOST. I lost the chance to teach, lost the chance to impact the hearts of the students, and lost the opportunity to create an environment of learning.

One day at the beginning of the marking period, I spoke to the entire class, who were sitting on the bleachers. I can't remember the topic, probably procedures on how to behave in my class. I remember one student being disrespectful, at least that was how it appeared to me. I couldn't believe he wouldn't give me his undivided attention. I called him out. I told him to stop talking or I would send him to the office. He ignored my statement, and he continued talking. I warned him again, and I received the reply, "I don't care." That was it. I wasn't going to look bad in front of the class, and I told him to head to the office. He said, "No I am not going." Finally, after yelling at him, "I don't care what you want. Get out." I left the gym to get help from the hall monitor. Then the student left the gym. I may have won the battle, but I certainly lost the war. I lost an opportunity to teach him, help him, and develop a healthy relationship with him from that point on. I regret the power struggles that occurred due to my early years. Why should the students respect and listen to me when they don't know me? It took me a while to realize that real teaching is not about power. It's about love, caring, and empathy.

What does this have to do with being a lawyer

One day when I was walking around the gym taking attendance and talking with my students at Levy Middle School, a seventh-grade student

Gloria asked me, "Why do I need to learn how to play soccer? I am going to be a lawyer." That was a great question in which I mumbled through an answer, so I wouldn't seem rude and appear to be ignoring her. This interaction was a game changer for me in my teaching career. She didn't hold the same importance for athletics and fitness as I did. She wasn't challenging my authority; it wasn't a power struggle filled with rebellion. She felt that changing into physical education clothes, getting sweaty, and learning how to play sports was not part of her future. When I thought about the question, she made a good point: after college, most people don't participate in team sports. Was there a larger reason for teaching physical education? How could I reach her, teach her, and make the subject relevant to her? If she had this question, how many of my other students did too? I wasn't even thinking about the character or life skills I could teach through my class! Another lost opportunity to impact a student.

Little too sarcastic

I attended a graduation party of one of my varsity soccer players. In the backyard on my player's deck a group of seniors were discussing being in my physical education class in middle school. One student turned to me and said, "I've never heard you say anything that wasn't sarcastic." As I laughed it off with the other students, I really felt like I was hit with a two-by-four upside the head. After hearing his comment all I could think of was, I would be remembered as a teacher who was sarcastic. I used sarcasm as one of my defenses. I kept students away from my heart. Sarcasm prevented me from loving students and being fully engaged in their lives. I needed more help learning how to teach with my heart than I realized.

Not there yet

I started incorporating some of the needed internal work and trying to teach with my heart in my physical education classes. Like a child in the back of the car who asks, "Are we there yet?," this experience showed me that I still had some traveling to do. One day in physical education class,

I was jogging during warmups with the students. I was jogging behind two boys, Charles and Marcus. I overheard their conversations, "I am not buying all this manhood stuff from Mr. Horan. He doesn't understand what is going on. We are just in the program to play ball and have fun with friends." This hit my pride, initially caused some anger, but eventually showed me that I had not completed the journey of inner transformation. I was not fully teaching with my heart. I still wasn't connecting and reaching the students in the way I hoped. This encounter rekindled the spark and prepared me for the next part of the journey.

I needed to reexamine these early lessons to find my truth, heal, and seek guidance I needed to teach in a more passionate manner. Successful teachers impact students with empathy. Great teachers use their hearts to help these precious students strive for success and greatness.

Just beginning to see

One of the key things that happened during this time was many conversations with one of my mentors on race and teaching Black and Brown boys. Graham taught with me for a few years and then became a Doctor of Education, teaching at Syracuse University. Being a man of color that did a tremendous amount of research on education, especially educating Black and Brown boys, he was tremendously knowledgeable in this area. He shared research with me about how youth are devalued by society. This started another journey to understand how race really impacts this population's education and life. This helped me start to recognize my own racial bias – a bias I previously didn't think I held. I began to dig down to another level of doing the internal work, not just for my healing, but to gain the empathy and compassion to engage and teach others.

Deposit daily

The positive relationships with students were built on action, love, and trust. I had an opportunity to move to a different school, H.W. Smith PreK-8. I knew in my heart that after Levy Middle School had closed and

I had been teaching in an elementary school for a few years I needed to be back in middle school. At this time, I wanted to make a real difference in the lives of my students. I didn't want to fail at reaching the hearts of the students. I hoped to make an impact and knew nothing short of truly loving others was the key.

There was a student named Rashad who was known to cause havoc in the gym for the other physical education teachers. I didn't teach him at the time, but saw him every day at my morning duty post. My job was to prevent students from getting off the bus and heading to a nearby coffee shop. I guess caffeine and education don't mix well for young students. Every day, Rashad's mother would drop him at the corner, and he would walk past me. I knew I would probably have to teach him in future years and decided that I would build my own relationship with him. Each morning, I greeted him with "Good morning" as he walked by my post. I found out from another staff member that his older brother was in Building Men. I asked him, "How is your brother? Is he playing basketball in high school?" Eventually, I started asking Rashad some simple questions to build a relationship. In the colder months we had short conversations. As the spring came along, there were several occasions when he would stop and talk.

Over the course of the year, we became better acquainted, and what I heard about him from the other physical education teacher didn't make sense. I couldn't understand how he was seen as having a behavior problem. I had come to know a respectful, young man that I talked with nearly every day. Was I missing something? Maybe I wasn't seeing the boy's real character.

For the next three years, I was fortunate to teach Rashad in physical education class, and he was one of my best students. I saw Rashad, not the predetermined poorly behaved student past teachers labeled. I learned the importance of putting in the time and energy to connect with him as a person, not a name in the grade book. He started to shine in the class, and he joined the Building Men Program. He did not join the program to play sports, but to belong to something greater than himself. He was my right-hand man for the next two years. Rashad kept score for me, completed community service projects, and attended every Building Men event. Daily deposits of love at the bus stop paid off great returns.

Energy is key

At H.W. Smith PreK-8 School, I was open to learning more lessons and wanted to continue to grow. One thing I didn't realize from the earlier years of teaching in the gym was the importance of positive energy. H.W. Smith was an extended learning time school. Each student had an enrichment class during the school day. I was given the opportunity to teach a Building Men enrichment class. I was able to learn about the importance of energy and love while teaching this class.

In the gym, it was natural to get hyped up, be full of energy, and play with the students. It was a part of being a physical education teacher that I really enjoyed. I would sweat through three shirts during a floor hockey day and enjoy playing silly kids' games like tag, flicker ball, and capture the flag. The classroom is a different animal. The physical environment doesn't lend itself to as much movement. The energy that needed to be brought was love. When I brought the love and showed a strong desire for each student to be successful, they could feel it in the lesson. It was great. When my energy was low or my personal life was taking my energy, the class didn't flow. It was as if the boys could feel the level of empathy and love I brought to class each day. Students deserve my best every day, there is never a second chance to love. I needed to put my students first every day!

My Lessons

I was taught to look at teaching and students through a different lens, How can I impact the students? These experiences changed the way and why I teach others. Instructional techniques and obtaining higher degrees are important, but ignoring my heart prevented me from teaching the whole student.

- Teaching is about the heart of my students
- My personal bias negatively affected my ability to connect
- Teaching from a position of power will leave students empty
- Teaching the whole student with grace, humility, and love
- Each student must feel the love and energy to learn

Your Turn:

If teaching is about the "heart" of your students, make time each day to get to know the kids in front of you. You can use this chart to help.

Students Name	Favorite Subject	Hobbies	Family

CHAPTER 5

A Coach

THERE WERE AREAS of my life that needed to be changed or overhauled before I would be able to help others in their journey of manhood. One area of change was in my approach to coaching and sports. All my life I had placed winning at a premium and tried to avoid losing at all costs.

Prior to the Building Men Program, when I coached or played sports, I had a problem with healthy competition: I needed to win for my selfish needs and affirmation. My worth and value as a person was tied to whether I won or lost. How I felt about myself was like a stock in the stock market that rose and fell daily, not due to trading but winning or losing. I found myself competing to win at everything. Even when I played students in PE class, I would try to win. I remember playing floor hockey because they needed an extra player. I played defense so the other students on my team could play offense and try to score. In actuality, I was defending as much as I was trying to score from the defensive half of the court. This value of winning and finding my worth through sports needed to change. What I had learned by doing a self-assessment of my coaching was that I was a transactional coach. A transactional coach uses the athletes and sport to gain personal status, identity, or worth. When you are a transactional coach your teaching and coaching is not about helping the athlete grow and develop, it's used for personal gain. Just like making a transaction at the bank, never putting in, always a withdrawal.

At an InsideOut Training in Maryland led by Joe Ehrmann, was the first time I looked at how the coaches I had in my life impacted my heart. This all-day training had me so excited about learning new ways to help my team and win more games. I registered out front, I grabbed a free coffee, and took a seat in a room full of 60 other coaches, discussing, asking questions, and having fun. The training started. I was ready to take notes and was thankful that I was here to learn. As we started doing exercises on how one coaches the heart of the athlete, I could feel the atmosphere in the room change. I could feel myself shrinking in my chair, feeling very alone. As I held back tears, I realized my unhealthy and damaging feelings about sports for the first time. To be honest I played and coached to get my emotional needs met.

As I began reflecting from the time I was growing up in elementary school throughout adulthood I would walk onto the basketball court with one purpose. The purpose was less about playing basketball and more about determining whether I was man enough. My manhood was decided daily on the basketball courts of Syracuse. Every game I won, my manhood was elevated. When I lost, I felt less than a man. It was not the fact that I lost that hurt, but rather the feeling that I would never measure up. I would wake up early the next morning and to practice because I felt like my masculinity was on the line. It was always more than a game. I carried this attitude with me into my coaching and teaching career. This truth tore at my heart strings as I remembered different times in which my emotions impacted my student athletes in negative ways.

This unhealthy view and the value I placed on competition was some of the negative internal baggage I transferred to my coaching. I tried to approach every season with a positive mindset, teach character, and motivate my athletes but my internal talk and warped values stifled my positive approach. I would be so frustrated when we were losing at halftime, I gave the same halftime talk for several games in a row. One player finally spoke up and said, "You say the same thing every game. Nothing changes." As I looked back upon my seasons as a varsity coach, my internal baggage came out in many forms and impacted the athletes in a negative way. I did not coach the athletes' needs and hearts.

When I started coaching, I obtained my knowledge base from watching other coaches and reading about champion coaches. I would watch basketball coaches yell and question the referee's call. I would imitate this behavior on the sidelines. I watched successful coaches kick players out of practice if they didn't work hard enough or send the whole team home. It saddens me to say I did this a few times in my career. In my opinion, most of the coaches I had in my athletic career did a good job, but few actually impacted my heart. I needed to be the next best coach and really win. I would study, read, and watch sporting events, all with the attitude of winning and one day coaching in a big-time program. It was years before I realized the real impact my coaching had on my heart, which in turn affected my student-athletes.

Lessons from coaching basketball and soccer

Through doing some self-reflection after the InsideOut Training and starting to get honest about my role as a coach as it relates to my players, I learned some important lessons that started to lay the groundwork for true transformation.

I realized that there was a big difference in my approach and style of coaching within the two sports I coached: basketball and soccer. The differences in the approach and style of coaching within each was the level of my emotional connection. The sports that I played competitively in high school came with a greater level of connection to my pride and a need to win. This need to win and emotional connection brought my unhealthy value of competition and over-the-top importance on winning to the coaching environment. This created a transactional coaching environment that was damaging to my athletes and far from the reason I went into coaching.

Looking back when I coached basketball and soccer, I was still emotionally attached to the need to win. This was a result of my need to win in my youth to feel like I was good enough. I brought a different energy and emotion because I felt I had to win to be a successful man. It took some assessment of my coaching to realize the need for change and to have the willingness to do the hard work to change my values, beliefs, and attitudes toward these two sports.

Modified boys soccer team

When I started my journey towards becoming "A" Man, I took a new approach when I stepped on the soccer field. It became a practice ground to teach young boys how to be "A" man. I reexamined old practice plans, looking at them from a new perspective. Did the practice plan help develop the player or was it only about my pride and winning? Did the practice plan develop the athlete's skills, as well as their character, and heart? In the area of character, was I intentional about its development or hoped it happened by the end of the season? I started to find ways to create a different culture where every player was valued. As my goal of coaching was different, I valued the players over my need to win. The team would spend time before each practice talking about character traits such as integrity, perseverance, commitment, and relationships.

During warmups, I checked in with the boys on how they were feeling. In drills, I changed up the friend groups to give each athlete an opportunity to work with different players and build friendships. We talked about current events in sports that dealt with the character of the players or teams. I would pause practice to point out examples of character and manhood. I would call a timeout during a game to highlight a teachable moment when I saw a display of manhood and character. I gave the boys homework assignments that dealt with their character development.

The new approach took the boys, and myself, a bit to get used to. As a coach, I was used to getting all the boys to work immediately, every minute accounted for either a drill, conditioning or scrimmage. Some boys had a hard time as they were not used to talking about character, manhood, and emotions. Some boys complained in the beginning, but as the season went on, they bought into the new coaching approach. Although some time during practice was dedicated to character and manhood development, the team played hard and won. As respect and trust for each other grew, they learned it was OK to rely on others. We became a better team, as I became a better coach.

As a modified player's skill and development are the most important, I decided not to cut any players. Most boys welcomed the idea of not having cuts and creating a team that welcomed all boys. The number of boys who wanted to play on the team grew as we didn't cut anyone. Some parents didn't like the fact that I wouldn't cut players and their sons' playing time decreased. These changes were put in place for the boys, not the parents. As the season continued, I had many great conversations with parents, opposing coaches, and teachers who watched my players work together and support each other, no matter the skill level.

Franks and beans

As I began to change to a coach who was more concerned about my impact upon my players than my needs, there was a change in the team culture. We started each practice with character talks, and each pre-game focused on the character trait of the week. I talked with the older players about leadership and spent time with the younger players helping them understand their roles on the team. Every teammate had a place. The players were valued as people with hearts versus players with talent. Everyone was important because of the personal qualities they brought to the table, and everyone was invited to the table.

I still had inside work to do as my pride didn't vanish instantly. My pride went up when the soccer team was on a three-year undefeated streak and crashed when I coached a basketball team that couldn't win a game. These seasons showed me room for growth in my coaching development. I continued to self-reflect, research, and talk with others about the changes that needed to take place in my heart, character, and spirit. I needed a transformation of my heart to become a coach that can impact others no matter the final score or record.

Looking back on the beginning of my transformational journey, the "franks and beans" game was a tipping point. The "franks and beans" game idea was taken from another coach. I was always on the lookout, trying to find ways to improve my coaching and be like other successful coaches.

The franks and beans game was an inter-squad scrimmage that took place on the day of the last soccer practice. The concept was to have the eighth graders play against the seventh graders. I told them that the winner of the game would have hot dogs at the end of the season party and losers would have baked beans. The last practice of the season had the typical pre-game banter and bragging prior to the franks and beans game. The first half went well, a very close game. The emotions started to rise as the seventh graders scored a few goals. By the beginning of the second half, the players were taking cheap shots at each other, trash talking, and then a fight almost occurred. We ended the game at the end of the third quarter and circled up to try to debrief on what had happened. The teammates were at odds with each other, and the team was fragmented. I wanted to restore some team unity as we had our final game the next day.

We were able to finish the season with a win, but I lost as a coach. I started the season with hearts to mold and love and ended up with hearts damaged. I had to stop coaching this way. I needed to put all ideas through a test of heart. Will this help the development of the hearts of the athlete? There had to be a way to develop manhood in and through sports. My internal work wasn't complete. More research and personal development were needed to become "A" man and coach. I found a better way to end a season.

Winning doesn't solve problems

One of the lessons I learned was that winning didn't solve all the relational problems within a team. The Syracuse City School District combined three schools to form the boys' modified soccer team. This brought a new dynamic, where boys who didn't go to the same school and didn't know each other were expected to work and play together. Not only were the boys from different schools, but from different parts of the city, from different cultures, backgrounds, and faith traditions. The fact that we won some games didn't automatically make these guys playing together feel like they were on one cohesive team or friends.

The problem of racism showed itself in ways that separated boys into cliques on the team. Though I tried several team building activities, there remained three different groups of athletes: white athletes from one school, Black athletes from another, and Black and refugee athletes from the third. They were respectful of each other most of the time, but you could tell they were no united team. Winning covered up the issue for a while, but the feelings of prejudice and fear were a reality.

The more time we spent before and after practice in communication, learning about each other's differences, and building relationships, the more this helped to create one team. The underlying issues started to reduce as I started emphasizing the importance of healthy masculinity and touching their hearts. We stressed the importance of relationships and created a team culture of togetherness in daily discussions. We learned about each other's cultures and struggles. This emphasis seemed to positively impact the young men, as they learned their teammates were more than the number on their jersey. As our hearts became open to embrace all boys, no matter the culture, etc., the team continued to heal and become healthy. This helped the boys learn about the struggles they were experiencing in our schools and as a team.

Letter to a friend of another color

In looking at the many different cultures and nationalities that made up the soccer team, I had all the boys write a letter to a friend of another race, ethnicity, or nationality. I read about this activity from Joe Ehrmann. They had one week to write the letter. Then, during practice, they shared their letter with the team.

After each practice, four to five players took turns reading their letters out loud. The more letters that were read, the more we started to hear common traits of friendship. The common theme of a different race, ethnicity, and nationality started to fade and the story of relationships came forward. The lessons we learned were about accepting others, compassion, common interests, and love. We spent time talking about what makes a true friend and teammate. One player shared his letter, and we soon knew the friend of another color he was talking about was sitting here on the team. I could feel the heart connection between the two as the letter was shared. He told us all about a time when his friend stood up for him in a crowd at school and how the friendship was important in helping him feel like he belonged. There was a different feeling among the team that day, a feeling of love and hope. The letters showed us how our lives were better and enhanced by embracing the unique gifts brought to us by different races, nationalities, and cultures. The activity brought our team closer as we saw that our team was stronger because we had players from different races, nationalities, and cultures.

Time out for coins

When I began coaching, I had an athletic director that found a cool idea from a coach in Nebraska. She gave us a short article about a team that gave their opponents a sportsmanship coin at the end of the game. The coach would single out a player on the opposing team that showed good sportsmanship. This coach had the team walk over and they presented the sportsmanship coin to the opposing team's player. At the time, I thought it was a good idea, but I was more concerned with winning, not character, so I didn't do anything with the coins she provided each coach.

When I started looking for ways to use sports to impact character and the hearts of young men, I remembered the coin idea and found the article. I rifled through my office and found some coins in my desk junk drawer. The A.D. gave all the middle and high school coaches sample coins that read, "high five." I started asking around to other coaches I knew to see if anyone had any more coins they were not using.

As a team, we decided to start handing out sportsmanship coins. We called them manhood coins. After an awkward beginning to this new tradition, it became part of the team's culture. The sportsmanship coins are awarded to a member of the opposing team to honor the competition. We want the players to see the competitor as someone who helped them play to their highest level, not someone to beat, humiliate, or destroy. The players honored the efforts and character of each other to show winning with humility and losing with grace.

At the end of the game we would huddle up to decide who gets the coin. When we determined who we would honor and why we selected that player, you could feel the positive energy rise. At first I would present the coins, but by mid-season we had various players do the presenting. The entire team would walk over to the opposing team's bench and gather in a circle. I would get the coach's attention and explain to the players the purpose of the coins. Our player would hand out the coin to the chosen player and explain why we are giving it to him followed by cheering. The players would give a handshake and sometimes hugs to the coin winner and my team would break into their cool down lap.

It was typical for the players to come up to me before the game asking for the opportunity to present the coin. Usually, sometime during the season, our team would say, "I wish other teams did the coins so I could win one." We started to take time outs during games, not to discuss strategy, but to discuss which player deserved the coin.

This tradition led us into many discussions on sportsmanship and manhood qualities. We discussed things like how you treat and honor your opponents. How do you react to players that use illegal tactics to gain an advantage? The importance of winning all the time versus sportsmanship. Can we learn valuable lessons from losing? We dealt with the emotional and heart side of playing the game and developed, me included, a healthier concept of winning and losing.

Bull ring

In the summer of my tenth year coaching modified soccer, I was given a book to read, *3D Coach: Capturing the Heart Behind the Jersey* by Jeff Duke. In the book, there are several activities with the goal of touching the heart of young athletes. One activity that resonated with me was what we called the Bulldog Ring.

Terry was an eighth grader on my soccer team, and he was, what many would call, a bully. He was the sneaky kind of bully that would terrorize the smaller boys. He was not angry and physically hurtful. He sought to show his dominance and control over seventh graders from a different school. Terry would regularly sneak up into a group of seventh graders and say something inappropriate in their conversation. He would bump into a teammate on purpose during the warmup run, take someone's cleats, call them names continually, and threaten the smallest boys behind my back. That season, I tried out the Bulldog Ring with the team.

Each day, a player would stand in the center of the circle and allow their teammates to say positive characteristics about them. These positive comments could not be related to their soccer skills or performance. It took a few tries for the boys to be comfortable giving and receiving compliments. Among our youth it is more common to hear disrespectful and degrading comments than uplifting, positive ones. This exercise helped us learn more about each other and gain a deeper understanding of talents, skills, and interests outside of soccer. The positive relationships among the members of the team grew. There was one outcome I didn't see coming.

When it became Terry's turn, I could see his hesitation. Terry may have anticipated negative comments from the boys as payback for his bullying behavior. What he expected didn't happen. The boys started saying all positive qualities Terry brought to the team and shared examples of the good qualities he had displayed during the season. I took the opportunity to talk with Terry about what happened and how these boys showed love despite his actions. From that day forward, he changed his behavior, stopped bullying, and became a positive member of the team. The boys helped Terry build positive team relationships from that day forward. When he lowered his defense mechanisms, he allowed himself to have friendships on the team.

Give first, receive second

At the end of the season, I wanted to finish in a positive manner and teach one more important lesson. Through my journey, I learned that for transformation to happen, I needed to give of myself and not expect anything in return. I would not be able to change my life if I was always looking for self-gratification and having a self-centered attitude. I could not have a positive impact without giving of myself freely. My mentor once told me that the joy of living is found in giving. I wanted to teach the boys about giving first and receiving second.

For the end of the year celebration, the tradition was to get together at one school, have some pizza and cake, and hand out awards. This year, I decided to have the team give to others first before they would eat and celebrate. We split the team up by the three schools they attended and gave each school a task. The players from one school brought the peanut butter, jelly, and bread; another school brought some water bottles; and the last school brought snacks and fruit to complete the bag lunch. All the boys did their best to contribute to the project even though some families lacked the financial ability to do so. During the season, most boys became aware of the teams' diversity, not just in race and ethnic groups, but in socio-economic status as well.

The bus brought the boys from the three different Syracuse City schools together Hughes Magnet School and Ed Smith K-8 came to H.W. Smith Pre-K-8, on the day of the party to make bag lunches for the homeless. We started by writing notes of encouragement to bring a smile and maybe touch the heart of the people in need. Some of the notes read, "Have a great day," "Keep the Faith," "God loves you," and other positive words of encouragement.

Traditionally in the Building Men Program we made sandwiches for the local men's homeless shelter over mid-winter break. Each February, we have a week break (mid-winter recess) from school, and I'd get the boys together to hang out, play some basketball, eat food, but more importantly, to do community service. When provided with the opportunity, boys are willing to give and do work for others. The older boys lead, serve, and teach the tradition to the younger boys. This tradition has been going on for over 12 years.

There were some Building Men boys on the soccer team who took the leadership role and set up the sandwich making and lunch bagging assembly line. Some had the job of peanut butter spreaders, others the jelly guys. Some players were bagging the completed sandwiches and others added the snacks to the brown bags while the last guys were on quality control. After completing the bag lunches, we discussed the problem of homelessness and poverty in our community. The boys asked "why don't the homeless get a job or a house?" We talked about the possible trauma, mental health issues, bad break, and racism that happens in our city. We discussed the importance of service, especially helping the disadvantaged. It is hard for the boys to understand how someone could have no one to help them.

After the discussion and answering many questions, we took all the lunches and water to the school bus. Prior to the celebration, the bus driver got permission to drive us around the city so we could hand out lunches and water to the homeless. As we drove around, the players took turns handing out the bag lunches and water bottles. We returned to the school for the party. Give first – receive second.

I now understand

After the celebration party was over and we started cleaning up, one of the eighth graders came up to me for what I thought was the typical "thank you, coach." He said, "Coach, I didn't really get why you spent so much time on all the manhood discussions when I first joined the soccer team in seventh grade. I now understand why you spent all the time discussing manhood. Thank you." This short conversation was the reason why I did all the reflection, prayer, and work with my mentors. I finally was able to be a coach of character instead of coaching only to win! I felt the need and desire to do more than coach the X's and O's of the sport. I wanted to provide our young boys the safe space to talk, learn, and reflect on the journey of manhood. When I was a teenager, I pretended that I knew all the answers, but I didn't even know the questions which needed to be asked. I didn't know what I didn't know. I was starting to turn the corner and create an environment of transformation.

My Lessons

I needed to look at my coaching philosophies, experiences, and practices. What was my definition of success, for me and for the development of the team? What are the core values of my coaching philosophy? Bottom line, am I a transactional or transformational coach? These were questions I examined. Below are the lessons I learned from doing my self-assessment and finding out how my experiences coaching not only impacted me but affected my athletes.

- Importance of examining the reasons why I coached
- A transactional coach gets their value from the players
- A transformational coach coaches to transform the hearts of the players
- Teaching character needs to be intentional
- Walk the talk; actions speak louder than words
- The sense of belonging needs to be cultivated and protected
- Need to investigate racial biases
- Take time to teach life lessons and manhood, as they will grow up to become men, not just athletes

Your Turn:

- How do your own athletic experiences shape the way you coach?
- Why do you coach?
- Are you a transactional or transformational coach?
- How do you define success in your professional life, personal life, and as a coach/mentor?
- What is your philosophy on "winning?"

CHAPTER 6

A (Family) Man

WHEN MY LIFE was rocked by the divorce, I questioned my masculinity and direction of my life. At this point, all I could see was my heart's desire to have a family fade away. I wasn't going to let that happen. I knew I needed help to figure out why I struggled with relationships. I was finally humbled enough to get help, and I sought out professional counseling. I began to see some of the truth I had been denying in my relationships with women. Looking to my peers, co-workers, social media or my family to find the answers would not help. I needed to begin the process of serious self-reflection to reexamine my beliefs, motives, and attitudes towards the opposite gender.

As I started this self-examination, I decided to return to my roots. I did this by going back to the church of my youth, St. Lucy's in Syracuse. I realized that by returning, there was a peace and comfort I would find in the community. Not only would I feel peace again, but I would find my new family.

I started counseling to heal from my divorce. I met a wonderful woman who happened to have an amazing son. I needed to change how I engaged in an intimate relationships. In past relationships, I would say what I thought she wanted me to say, leave out how I was feeling, and not tell the whole truth. My relationships were based on a fear that she wouldn't like me or would break up with me. I was determined to get honest, change my attitudes and behaviors, and have a family. I worked on getting over the lie of having to be the best and greatest. I was humbled by life and wanted to be "A" man.

At St. Lucy's there was a children's ministry in which the younger children would have the time to learn about God downstairs in the basement during the mass. Just before the readings and reflections, the priest would ask all the children to come forward for a blessing. The young children of all ages, sizes, and cultures would crowd around this beautiful woman, their teacher, awaiting the blessing. To me, there was nothing more beautiful than this young woman, surrounded by all these beautiful children receiving the blessing from the church community. Every Sunday, I would watch with awe as she awaited the blessing to be prepared to teach these kids, one of which happened to be her son.

Finally, I found my truth, the type of intimate relationship I was looking for in my life. She had something special that made her glow. It was the beauty in her heart. It was like I could see her heart, a heart that cared for the children. She was sharing God and love to these children each week. There was no question my heart was yearning for this type of relationship.

One Ash Wednesday after mass, I was hurting and felt the need for extra prayer. I stayed in the back of the church to pray for a bit, hoping for some relief. In the middle of prayer, I looked up and I saw her walking down the aisle towards the back of the church. She must have forgotten something. At that moment I said to myself, "I'm going to marry her someday."

A few Sundays later, I needed to leave church early to coach an indoor soccer game. I waited in the back for her to come up after teaching children's ministry. I asked her if she'd like to have coffee sometime. This started a friendship that turned into a relationship based on honesty, faith, and love. A year and a half later we were married.

MaryPat was the better teacher

In my continued search to become a better teacher and coach, one that teaches with heart, I was given a new teacher. The new model teacher came when I got engaged to be married to MaryPat. MaryPat was a very dedicated mother to Zac, and she started to teach me how to give of myself to others. I had much to learn about giving my time, talents, and love to others and how love impacts their lives.

In the fall before we were married, Zac was interested in playing soccer. MaryPat, while an amazing mother, was never the best physical education student in school. Even though she lacked the knowledge about soccer, she volunteered to coach her son's soccer team because no other parents stepped up. This required her to research how to coach four to six-year-old boys that had endless amounts of energy. My mind went back to a question that Gloria asked during my physical education class, "Why do you need to learn physical education if you want to be a lawyer?" The answer, in this case, was you need to know how to be your son's soccer coach.

I watched her coach these young children from her heart. The practice sessions were more about playing games to have fun, get exercise, and laugh. This team was not about intense soccer skills training. The practice ended with a check on how everyone felt, cheers, high fives, and announcements. She was the most encouraging coach I have watched, as she walked, jogged, and sometimes broke into a quick run up and down the field talking with her players. The time-outs at the end of each quarter were not spent talking strategy, as I thought it should, the breaks were about snacks, juice boxes and checking in on how they were doing and feeling. She helped them in every aspect, from teaching them their positions, showing them how to have fun, providing great snacks, and cheering on the team. She didn't care more about winning than having fun, nor was she concerned with proper skill development, she cared for their hearts. This experience started to change my heart, and I became the assistant coach of Zac's soccer team that year.

This experience transformed my mindset of being a coach and a father. At first, I thought this was pretty much the same role, but my wife was good at reminding me when to take the coaching hat off and be a dad.

I needed to change how I spoke to Zac as a dad and not always be a coach. The change needed to happen in my heart, not just my head. I learned how to father and coach from the heart, with love. Through many mistakes and false starts, I learned when he needed my encouragement, love, and support as a father, not to harp on the techniques and effort he showed in the games as a coach. He needed to know that I always believed in him and his greatness no matter the outcome of the game. A good father would value his son's efforts and guard his heart no matter what transpired on the soccer field. In learning this lesson about being a good father, could I give others that same kind of love and encouragement as a coach?

Not only did my wife impact my coaching with Zac, she also impacted how I coached the boys on the modified soccer team. I started to realize, by looking within and being honest with myself, my dream of becoming a successful coach, one that just won, wasn't my calling. Thankfully, I finally learned to coach boys into young men, not only soccer players.

My son, my why

My approach to teaching and coaching continued to change as Zac and I grew closer. I had this longing to be a dad, to have a special bond with my own son. At the same time, I was scared that I might fail as a father. Here I was an instant father to a 5-year-old, and I never received the parent manual. I knew my struggle with my past relationships, and I didn't want to fail Zac. I was on this journey to learn how to become a man, and knew I needed to learn how to teach Zac to become one, too. There was no advance training. I felt that I was alone and had to figure it all out. I spent years teaching and coaching middle school boys, but there was some fear in parenting a 5-year-old. I needed to push these fears aside and seek help on this journey.

My son really started to push me harder on the journey to be "A" man. The overriding question, thought, and motivation at this time was, "If I do not know how to become "A" man, how can I teach Zac?" This became the thesis statement for the next decade of work.

My research on manhood popped up in every area of my life. I couldn't learn fast enough, and I made many mistakes along the way. Mentors and friends would email me suggestions of books to read. After reading a few books by super bowl winning coach Tony Dungy, I was introduced to an organization called All Pro Dad. This company is a fatherhood program that inspires fathers to be the best dad, husband, and person they can be. These daily emails from All Pro Dad taught me many lessons. I sought out conversations with friends and mentors who had children. This knowledge and these experiences provided me with different tools and started a transformation in my heart as I strived to be a better man and impact the hearts of young men. The internal journey and the experiences which changed my relationship with Zac manifested a change with my students in my classes and my athletes on the field.

Opportunities

My biggest motivation wasn't to improve my life as much as I wanted to give my son the best upbringing and instill in him the values that would help him be successful. I wanted him to be exposed to different people, cultures, and lifestyles, to help him learn more about the world in which we live. I wanted to provide him with opportunities and experiences to help him make quality choices and decisions.

I started having him join in with Building Men activities, like open gyms, sandwich making for homeless, care package making for soldiers, and community clean ups. He would join in and play ball with the boys, and he attended a few field trips as well. Zac made chili for the homeless shelter and asked family and church members to donate socks and scarves to bring down to the shelter.

As a result of the growth of Building Men, Zac and I had opportunities to visit colleges and businesses, and participate in service projects across the city. This gave him greater exposure and opportunities that led to a variety of discussions to help him find his passion and purpose in this world.

Developing empathy for others

One of the hard aspects of teaching is not knowing the backstory of the students who are sitting in front of you. I have attended a variety of professional development sessions including teaching students with different behavioral challenges, classroom management techniques, and developing strategies to help students on different social and emotional tiers. When I started teaching, I heard many stories of the trials so many children go through in their homes and communities. I began to think about how it impacts their ability to learn. I learned this information intellectually, but it was hard for me to believe in my heart when I didn't have a frame of reference. I had the experience of teaching students and coaching athletes who seemed to have something going on in their head and heart that impacted them in education and sports. Suddenly, they would just check out, act out, or walk out. It was my son who helped me understand why.

Zac had some early childhood trauma in his life before I married his mother and became his father. Being in his life daily, I would see first-hand how situations he experienced earlier in his life continued to impact him years later. I watched him work through anger when he experienced a situation that triggered a past emotion. He didn't have a predetermined plan on when this emotional trigger or anger would occur, it just happened. Its impact was powerful. I noticed my son's mood would change instantly, and intense emotions rose to the surface. Why would I expect my son to act as if nothing happened and all was great in life? How could I expect my students to not be impacted if they had experienced trauma? He spent years healing from the trauma he experienced in the first seven years of his life. I am so very proud of him for doing the internal work and getting the help from counselors and mentors.

I started to notice the same experiences happening with some of my students and athletes. During the school day, a trigger could occur. In school, a place where we expect students to learn, an instant shift forces students to deal with feelings of hurt, anger, and various emotions. If these emotions are not dealt with at the time, the student would repress these feelings and emotions without a way to defuse or understand their origin. At some point the repressed emotions will come to the surface.

This brought my teaching to a new level of empathy. I needed to learn and understand what they might be going through. It wasn't the student that needed to learn more and change, it was me. I needed a better understanding about trauma-informed teaching, learning, and healing.

I realized that I needed to find a way to help them, love them, and create a safe environment. I started to understand the impact trauma had on students' learning, behaviors, and relationships. Learning this helped me be a more empathetic teacher and coach. The importance of getting help for childhood trauma is not widely accepted. A stigma remains for those who seek help with mental health problems. These children need healing for the trauma they didn't cause but were impacted by daily.

How can I teach manhood?

A question that continued to come to the surface was how could I teach Zac to be a man while I was in the process of healing my own masculinity? I continued researching the subject of manhood, fatherhood, and coaching young men to manhood. I looked for ways to inspire and engage Zac in conversation about masculinity. I worked on examining my approach to teaching and coaching under the new lens of authentic masculinity, love, and empathy. Zac became the test pilot for my new ideas.

Zac and I started his manhood training when he was in sixth grade. This was also the grade in which he would have started his experience in Building Men. We held manhood meetings on Sunday nights, around the fireplace outside or in our breezeway during bad weather. We read about warriors, chivalry, and knights of old. I used videos from motivational speakers like Eric Thomas and movie clips from the classics like *"Rudy,"* *"Remember the Titans,"* *"Finding Forrester,"* and *"Antwan Fisher"* and books like *"Touching Spirit Bear"* to talk about being a man. Trying different ideas and concepts to challenge his thinking and offer new ideas about being "A" man was part of the approach.

The goal was to help him develop into the best version that he was created to be. I tried to figure out how I connected with this special young man to teach him how to be "A" man, not "the" man. There were many times my wife would let me know when I missed the mark. All these lessons would be the beginnings of developing the Building Men Program, a way to teach the boys at school how to become "A" man.

There is significance in developing ceremonies to celebrate different stages in life and levels of achievement. In our society there are ceremonies for sports seasons, levels of school, and certain levels of success that are achieved. I experimented with different ways to honor Zac's efforts to motivate him as he worked towards stages of manhood. I developed a system that used the image of a knight's shield that would serve as a checkbox system when he was of service to others. For other stages, he earned chainmail body armor and a sword for different birthdays.

Exposure

Zac and I connected with some amazing men that helped us with service projects and opportunities for mission trips. At every service project, a new manhood concept would arise for discussion. Zac learned the importance of giving to others and not judging others based on the circumstances of their lives. These service experiences were within our own city, but opportunities started to open for us to travel to other parts of the country and overseas. This exposed Zac to authentic men and brought him a wide range of experiences to open his eyes to authentic masculinity. By seeing the bigger picture, it helped us develop greater empathy and compassion for our fellow man. Zac was more willing to stand up for the friend being picked on and shunned by the popular kids. He continued to fight for the underdog throughout high school and into early adulthood. One of the best ways we have learned to grow is to give to others without expecting anything in return.

While I would love to tell the story that these experiences had an immediate and full impact on Zac leading him to a life of success, this was not the case. Like all of us, his journey had many bumps and bruises. Some of the lessons during service trips were not revealed to him until in his early 20s. These lessons planted a seed within Zac's heart which continues to grow to this day! I believed what worked with my son could work with the Building Men boys. As a result of the research and experiences which helped Zac develop as a young man, the experience of service projects/trips shaped his view of manhood.

A Runner

While I focused most of my attention and my heart on being dad to Zac, I started to see a change in my teaching physical education at Hughes Elementary School. Levy Middle School was closed by the Syracuse City School District and I had an opportunity to move to Hughes Elementary School. I was used to teaching middle school grades, but I now had many different elementary grade physical education classes. As this new experience began, I started teaching with a different frame of reference. Each day when I looked at these children, I reminded myself that I was teaching my son.

In situations where a student would shut down or start crying, I would be baffled. I didn't know the reason why, and I was unaware of which situation triggered this reaction. I would approach the situation as if these students in my class were my son or daughter.

One day I remember when one of my second-grade students ran out of my class, I reacted differently. The old Joe would chase him down and do some power and control move to get him back to class. This day, I stopped for a moment and thought about a time Zac ran into his room and slammed the door. Something happened that triggered a past traumatic experience, and he reacted. At that moment, yelling would not provide comfort to what he was experiencing. He needed someone that was patient and loving to help him return to a calm mental state. What I learned from helping Zac allowed me to support this student by being a loving parent, not a controlling teacher. The change was developing relationships with the students as well as understanding their needs. While this can take extra time, the rewards are great. I started asking the students more questions about their lives and became more invested in getting to know them individually, not a group of kids in my class. This same student who ran out of the gym has been in my life for the last 11 years and is currently a senior in high school. We speak and see each other regularly. Our relationship has continued to grow and he is growing into an amazing young man. By learning to see the seed of greatness within a student, not the behavior of the student, this new perspective has changed how I teach and coach.

If I want to impact others, I need to view them as my own and not as random students. I asked myself, how would I teach, nurture, and discipline my son? Many of my students were dealing with trauma. I needed to react out of love. I spent more time nurturing relationships with each student. My emphasis was on building relationships first, getting my lessons done second. With this new basis of thinking, it helped me to change my teaching.

I started to teach from a place of love and caring not a position of power and privilege. This changed how I treated and spoke to students. I found that my teaching now came more from my heart, not my head. I evolved into the best version of myself. Although I still made mistakes, I realized I couldn't stop checking my heart.

My Lessons

My family changed and shaped how I taught and coached. The experiences of being a father changed my mindset and made me look at life through a different lens. Here are some of the takeaways from my self-assessment and finding out how my experiences as a dad influenced my work and personal life.

- Doing the internal work on my trauma in life helps me relate to others

- The students I teach and coach are my students – chosen for me to love and nurture
- Trauma in students impacts their ability to learn
- Teaching and coaching with compassion and empathy produced great results
- Students need opportunities and exposure to grow into the best versions of themselves
- Teachers and students are on the journey together, a positive relationship is essential

Your Turn:

- How do you reset and gain balance in your life?
- If you are a parent, think about the way this has influenced you as an educator.
- If you are not a parent, think about your relationships with your students/athletes; are they treated the way you would want your future child to be treated? Why or why not?

CHAPTER 7

Building Relationships

THROUGH TEACHING, COACHING, and creating the Building Men Program, I was spending most of my time talking about the importance of relationships. We talk about being a complete man, physically, mentally, socially, and in spirit. In the early days of Building Men in my heart I knew I would never be a complete man until I addressed my relationships with women. This area of my life still needed an overhaul if I was going to be able to guide and help others. I have been blessed with many lessons and am grateful for patient teachers.

My experiences with intimate relationships, before MaryPat were not successful. I needed to do an inventory on my attitudes, biases, and past relationships. With the help of professional counseling, I examined my unhealthy relationships I had had in my early 20s, my failed first marriage, and being a father. The relationships I previously had were immature and based on meeting my needs. I remember dating a young lady in college who wanted a healthy relationship. She wanted to go for walks, talk on the phone, and get to know each other and enjoy our time together. She wanted to spend less time watching movies and more time talking about our interests and thoughts. While I wanted to go to bars, she wanted a nice quiet dinner to talk. After a few weeks, I broke up with her. I did not have a reason. I simply couldn't handle the demands of a healthy relationship. I wasn't mature enough or held the right mindset to have a healthy relationship at that time.

I needed to examine the unhealthy views and attitudes I held towards the other gender. What changes did I need to make to have real heart-to-heart relationships based on love? What did I need to learn to have an honest relationship based on trust, communication, and respect? These seemed like the hardest lessons for me to unpack.

Not only was I struggling with my internal condition, but I was in a battle with the systemic teaching and cultural views about women and society's messages of masculinity. This led me on a journey to find my truth, my view of women and gender norms. As I found my truth, there was a need and desire to help others in their journey. This was my uphill challenge, sometimes a painful one, to change the way I teach, coach, and mentor young men.

Whopper

Out of respect for my first daughter's mother, I agreed to visit my daughter when she chose to see me. Any type of relationship would be on her time-table, not mine. As you could imagine, this left a longing in my heart. The first time I saw my daughter since she was an infant was a divine meeting.

In November 1993 before snowfall, I was supposed to get new tires. After looking around for the best prices, I found a good deal at the Sears in Camillus Mall. On Monday, I scheduled an appointment for Saturday, November 13th in the afternoon, not ideal but the only available time slot. On Wednesday, my friends voted me the host of the SU vs. Virginia Tech football game party on Saturday. I jumped at the opportunity to host. I started planning the menu and getting ready to prepare some food, then I remembered the car appointment. I quickly canceled my appointment with Sears and rescheduled for the following Tuesday, November 16th.

Tuesday around 4:00 p.m., I was walking around Camillus Shopping Mall waiting for my tires to be put on. I am not a shopper. My routine: go in, make your purchase, and get out. Just walking around looking at different stores and trying on a bunch of clothes was not enjoyable. It was about 5:00 p.m. and I was getting hungry, and the flame broiled burgers smelled great. I stopped into Burger King for my favorite, the No. 1, a whopper meal. Mind you, I have only been to Camillus Shopping Mall a few times in my life and never on a Tuesday afternoon. While sitting there eating the Whopper and fries, my daughter's mother came into the restaurant with her three children, one being my daughter. It has been over six years since I was able to see my daughter. We said hello to each other, and she asked if she could sit down and join me. I was nervous, but agreed. They all sat down with me, and for the first time in my life, I couldn't finish eating a Whopper. My heart was in my stomach. As we spoke, I found out that she remarried, and my daughter was part of a wonderful family. This brought me some relief knowing that my daughter was well taken care of. My daughter didn't know I was her biological father, I couldn't keep my eyes off her. She was so beautiful. Her mother and I continued to talk for a while, then she got a snack for her kids, and we went our separate ways. This encounter sparked the deep desire within to be a father years before Zac and MaryPat came into my life.

Girl's coach — why?

In 1992, I first worked at Levy Middle School, I was a teacher assistant in a special education classroom for children with autism. During one early spring, I kept hearing an announcement, "We are looking for someone to coach the girls' modified softball team, if you are interested, please contact the Physical Education department." At first, I ignored the announcement because I was a man and never thought of coaching girls' sports. After a week of hearing the announcement, I decided I would volunteer. I wanted to be a physical education teacher, so maybe this could be a foot in the door for a job somewhere in the district. I started coaching middle school girls' softball. I never played organized baseball as a kid, and I never imagined I would be coaching girls.

After the first season of softball, they were looking for a girls' soccer coach for the fall. Yup, that coach ended up being me. This began my coaching career, as I coached girls' soccer and softball for the next 13 years and even one season of girls volleyball. I really enjoyed the years coaching girls. I moved up the coaching ladder, from modified to junior varsity to varsity over the course of the next seven years, with a special group of girls. I would spend time working with these girls doing all I could to help the program grow and be competitive against other schools. I started running soccer clinics, coaching indoor soccer in the winter, and offering soccer camps in the summer. During the spring in the evening I began holding softball pre-season practices and I would even drive some girls to softball pitching and hitting clinics.

I was devoted to helping these girls win and succeed. I can't say I was the best coach during this time, but I loved my girls and would do anything to help them. We had car washes, held garage sales, worked concession stands, and sold Gertrude Hawk chocolate candy.

After my 13-year coaching career, I resigned from coaching girls' sports to devote my time to creating a Building Men Program and coaching boys' sports. One day after the final girls' soccer season, I realized where this passionate desire to coach girls' sports came from, my daughter. I started coaching modified girls' softball and soccer when she turned 6 and continued until she turned age 20. For 13 years, the drive, passion, and energy I poured into coaching came from my heart. When I look back upon those years, I couldn't be a father to my first daughter, so I fathered others.

I finally realized the impact my first daughter had on my teaching and coaching. I was able to use my pain, love, and yearning for my daughter to teach, coach, and love the girls in my classes and teams. Those 13 years of my life were a divine mission I never fully realized.

My blessing, Clare

Before MaryPat and I got married, we agreed that we might be getting too old to have children together. I was good with this agreement because I had a family with MaryPat and Zac. Shortly after the wedding, MaryPat and I discussed having children again, and we decided to try for six months. In two months, we were pregnant and nine months later we were blessed with Clare. I had no idea the change having Clare would have on my heart.

Being Clare's dad taught me many new lessons. I learned patience in the early mornings, how to walk laps around the dining room table to put her to sleep, and gained a wealth of knowledge about the Disney princesses. I started learning how the environment impacts a child, and the importance of creating a safe space to explore and learn. When she started to learn how to walk, I saw first-hand the importance of failures and developing new strategies. When she felt safe, I could see in her eyes that there was nothing she was unwilling to attempt, even trying all the things that her older brother Zac was doing. She would go right out onto basketball courts and soccer fields without fear: she belonged.

I often thought about how society devalues girls, and how the world treats women as less than a man. I wondered how this would impact Clare as she grows. Will my precious daughter be a victim one day of sexual/domestic violence and be marginalized by society? I needed to take a deeper look at my biases, values, and mindset as it pertains to women, and ask how these views will influence the work with the Building Men boys.

How do men treat women?

In reflecting on the current data of the number of women in our community that are impacted by sexual and domestic violence, the chances of Clare being sexually assaulted and raped were high! At this time, I started a new journey to learn about sexual and domestic violence prevention programs.

The Syracuse City School District offered Mentors for Violence Prevention (MVP) training to all coaches in the district. The training was facilitated by a national organization based out of Boston, MA and supported through Vera House Inc. in Syracuse, New York.

Vera House provides services in the areas of counseling, advocacy, emergency shelter, and prevention education, that touch thousands of individuals each year. Vera House provides comprehensive and compassionate care to those suffering from domestic violence, sexual abuse, and elder abuse. Vera House has domestic/sexual violence prevention programs called Men Lead By Example and Engaging Men & Boys. These programs encourage men and boys to work as allies with women and girls to prevent domestic and sexual violence and create healthy relationships. The Engaging Men & Boys Program provides opportunities for boys and men to engage in leadership conversations, challenge assumptions, and change cultural norms that allow violence to occur.

The MVP program was described to the coaches as a peer leadership program where the athletes would become leaders in the school. My thinking was "this is fantastic, my athletes would get this peer leadership training and become leaders who can impact the school." I jumped right in and signed up for the training. I had no idea what I was jumping into.

Much to my surprise the majority of the MVP training was not about how to train your athletes to be peer leaders, but how to get student athletes to stand up about issues of sexual assault, rape, and domestic violence. In the training, we discussed:

- How men value women
- How society and the world view women as inferior
- How men treat them as a material possession
- Why men feel that they have the right to abuse women

What I learned in the training hit me hard! The impact of domestic and sexual violence can have on women and families was described in detail. The facilitators brought us through activities and discussions that opened my eyes to the way I devalued women. These discussions made me reexamine the value I place on women and homosexuals. I experienced a tremendous amount of guilt and shame about my attitudes towards women and the fact that I didn't take a stand earlier in my life to prevent sexual and domestic violence.

Then I started to hear about the different types of trauma women and children experience during incidences of domestic violence. My thoughts went straight to MaryPat and Zac. My heart broke. I couldn't imagine the family I love going through such a traumatic experience. As I started to gain a better understanding of the trauma and experiences that my wife and son lived through, I became overwhelmed.

Hearing how these violent experiences impacted and scarred my wife put me in crisis mode, and I shut down. One of the facilitators noticed that I was dealing with some emotional issues. He tried to speak with me, but it didn't help. I was done with this program. I checked out, just like students would do in class when things got too hard.

A flood of questions came into my mind: What hurt and pain was my wife still dealing with because of the abuse? To what level of trauma was Zac still experiencing? What type of future will MaryPat and Clare have in a world that devalues women? And what would happen if Clare ended up being abused, and would my daughters ever be raped? After a few weeks of not being able to shake these thoughts, I started talking with my mentor. We discussed what could happen if I ignore this problem. I needed to face these issues if I ever planned on creating a better future.

I felt like I needed to change my community and world, but first I needed to change myself. I needed to have hard conversations about my attitudes, beliefs, and biases concerning women and gender. This journey led me back to Vera House.

The 12 Men Model

A result of attending the MVP training, I was contacted by Vera House as a follow-up to the training. One Vera House facilitator encouraged me to participate in a program called the "12 Men Model." I didn't like the idea of attending another one of these training sessions after the experience with MVP. I knew I had unfinished business in my heart concerning this matter of relationships with females.

For the "12 Men Model," I was commissioned to recruit 12 of my friends and colleagues to participate in a workshop to discuss how we view women, relationships, and domestic and sexual violence.

I talked with some friends and co-workers about participating; I came up a bit short, but I had eight guys join me for the five-hour workshop. During this program, we dug deeper into what I started to learn and experience in MVP. Doing this internal work on gender inequality and sexual violence was like peeling an onion, there were so many layers. The "12 Men Model" taught me how society pushes men to have relationships based on dominance and power. Often, in groups like these, men relate to situations in their lives where relationships were based on power and control. Many of the eight men in the group were engaged and impacted by the conversation. They shared their past relationships that were based on power and control and even the number of women they knew were abused. This opened further discussions on the topic of toxic masculinity. A few men dug deeper by continuing on their own personal journeys.

I started to connect the dots between the different training sessions with Joe Ehrmann, MVP, and "12 Men Model." The internal work to recognize the messaging and damage in my past needed to be healed before I could be an effective husband, father, teacher, and coach. As I continued having conversations with my mentors, wife, and professionals, my heart started to change and my eyes began to open. These topics needed to be shared with the boys at an earlier age than 47, if they were to bypass the pain and trauma I experienced. How could I teach this subject to young men in middle school? Was there a program available to engage young men in these hard, but important, conversations?

Healthy Masculinity conference

Talking one day with the facilitator of the "12 Men Model" from Vera House, he mentioned he had attended a Healthy Masculinity Conference in Washington, D.C. The three day conference is designed to create emotionally healthy leaders in the areas of relationships with women and girls to bring an end to gender based violence. The facilitators helped construct a healthy view of masculinity through presentations, videos, and role play exercises. He encouraged me to check it out. After talking with my wife, we decided that I should continue my journey. I traveled to Washington, DC. To attend the conference hosted by Men Can Stop Rape.

This turned out to be a huge internal challenge for me as I tried to keep an open mind and heart for all three days. Memories of the MVP Training came to mind along with experiences I learned from my wife and son. I didn't want to close down again when talking about topics of abuse, gender differences, and masculinity. I needed to deal with the internal biases head-on. If I didn't learn and grow, the potential of losing my wife and being emotionally unavailable in other relationships was great. How many times was I willing to ignore the inner work?

I met some amazing people from all around the country that helped me learn about healthy and authentic masculinity. A connection was made with others doing the work to stop sexual and domestic violence. We discussed unhealthy masculinity; the dominant story told to us by society. The dominant story is a cultural narrative told by the money-making media industries propagating views of women and minority groups as merchandise, not people. We took an in-depth look at the destructive messages that women are here for the pleasure of men, an object to be owned, and used by the privileged in our society. We discussed groups and individuals who are oppressed by racism and gender issues. We examined how different communities, like the LGBTQ+ community, were being treated, oppressed, and threatened with physical and emotional abuse daily. An older woman spoke to me about how elderly people were viewed as "less than" in our society. The conference was filled with stories of devaluing people and how to prevent, teach, and stand up for the rights of all. This was an eye-opening conference that showed me I needed to work on my internal prejudices. Part of this work, for me, was standing up for the rights of others and bringing this knowledge back to Syracuse.

MOST club

At the Healthy Masculinity Conference, I asked one of the facilitators how do you teach healthy masculinity to middle and high school boys? What type of program do you use when working with the young men in Washington, D.C.? He introduced me to Jay who runs the Men of Strength clubs (MOST club) in Washington D.C. The Men of Strength curriculum was developed by Men Can Stop Rape, the organization that put on the Healthy Masculinity Conference. They had great success engaging young men in conversations on masculinity through their curriculum. There are many MOST clubs in urban areas across the country. We had a great discussion about his experience running the MOST club. The MOST club sounded like the perfect program to be included in Building Men to help our young boys.

Upon my return to Syracuse, I started a conversation with Vera House about partnering to bring a MOST club to Syracuse. Through grant writing and collaboration, we successfully raised the needed funding to purchase the program. The Men Can Stop Rape staff came to Syracuse for a three-day training for staff of Vera House and Building Men.

Our staff learned, discussed, and brainstormed on different ways to engage our boys in conversations about masculinity. We looked at the dominant story of masculinity, the counter story of masculinity, relationships, violence, and bullying. The training provided us tools to help our young men do their internal work in these areas. This would create a safe and healthy space where our young men could come together to discuss manhood and grow into the best version of themselves.

We participated in an activity The Real Man, an activity in which the boys needed to pick between two celebrities and ask, "Who is The Real Man?" For example, the boys picked Lebron James because he was the best athlete, Jay Z because he was wealthy, or President Barack Obama because he had power. Doing this activity helped the boys evaluate perceptions society holds about being the real man.

The follow-up activity was to share about men in their life. We asked each boy, "Who is the strongest man you know?" We wrote down the character traits that made them the strongest. For example, the boys shared how their grandfather protected the family, how their dad provided for their family or how an uncle taught them how to care about themself. Over 85% of the time I did this activity, one boy would say his mother was the strongest man he knows. The boys would all relate to, not only the power and strength of our mothers, but the lack of strong males in their lives. We wrote down a list of character traits not specific to men, but high quality characteristics held by all human beings. We all have the strength and character to create change in our world. Everyone has value! The more I was able to look within and self-assess as a man, the more I learned how to help the boys and see their need for Building Men.

My Lessons

The social construct around gender influences our relationships with other people. This journey has been uncomfortable at times, as it contradicts what I grew up being taught. As I find the truth, I can teach with my heart and impact the lives of others. Here are a few lessons I learned from relationships and experiences that shaped me and changed my attitudes towards gender equity.

- The view and value of women impacted the way I taught and coached girls
- The disparities between men and women in sports affect equity, opportunity, and equality
- My privilege has blinded me from the larger problems in society
- Inequality and abuse of women is a man's issue, we need to take steps to fix the problem
- Our students need a safe space to discuss and reflect on the gender issues affecting society today

Your Turn:

- How has your upbringing and current view of women's rights impacted your relationships?
- Can you think about biases or stereotypes that you carry with you that define gender roles?
- What are your views surrounding gender equality?
- Are your views of women and gender issues set in stone or have they changed?
- What steps do you take to build a safe space to discuss larger societal issues?

CHAPTER 8

Unpacking Race

THERE WAS ANOTHER internal journey I needed to take to open my heart to the boys I was mentoring. I needed to take a deeper dive into race. To honestly examine how race influenced my perceptions of the students I taught, coached, and mentored. As a result of living in the inner city, I assumed that I knew how race impacted my life and the lives of the people in my community. Being a white male of privilege, I thought I had a handle on race, and I was doing enough by considering myself antiracist. Thanks to the men in my life, I was shown the depth of my racism. I was taught about privilege and how I would never fully know what it meant to be Black.

Building Men staff & the "12 Men Model"
The Building Men Program partnered with the Vera House to receive a grant to do some domestic and sexual violence prevention work with our young men in middle and high school. Building Men needed to complete our obligations for a grant we had partnered in with Vera House. As the grant time period was about to end, we were required to get more Building Men staff to participate in the "12 Men Model" program. Vera House agreed that I should be trained as a "12 Men Model" facilitator and facilitate the Building Men Summer Institute staff as my first group.

We went through the five-week sessions with ten Building Men Program staff and with each passing week the discussion became deeper and more intense. We were about to close the fifth session, and the facilitator from Vera House suggested we continue the conversation over a few more weeks. I agreed this training provided a good space for men to talk about topics we normally avoided. As we got to know each other better, the level of sharing deepened as our relationships grew. Just before the last week of the summer discussions, George Floyd was murdered and protests on racism erupted across the country. During our next session, we started our normal procedure of checking in with each other, one of the Black and Brown men in the session asked, "All right white guys, what are you going to do? It's (racism) your problem to fix."

I was taken aback by the honesty and directness in which that question was posed. My normal response to what I perceived to be a confrontational situation, would be to avoid and run. Instead, I tried to stay present and process my internal thoughts. Initial reactions that ran through my head were: ignore it, get angry, and how can he have blamed me? As I fought my natural instincts the question sunk in, and the anger subsided. What remained was the thought that I needed to do more to support our community's young Black and Brown boys. I knew I needed to take a deeper look at race and racism.

During the conversation, one of the men told us that it isn't the job of the Black and Brown community to teach us about racism. I knew I needed to start educating myself on the impact race played in my life, especially on how I taught, coached, and mentored the boys. Shortly after the "12 Men Model" session, I started talking with my mentors and researching my history with race. Within a week, I received an email invitation to attend a session on dealing with race by "InsideOut Coaching" and Joe Ehrmann. During the session Joe shared about writing his race-coherent narrative; I knew I had to do the same.

To process how race still impacts my life, I needed to record my experience with race. I took a look back on the times race influenced my relationships and experiences. The same internal work and self-assessment I did in the areas of masculinity and relationships, needed to be done with racism.

Roosevelt Junior High

The first memory of race was all the way back in fourth grade when I lived on the south side of Syracuse. At that time, there was a school called Roosevelt Junior High. Geographically, Roosevelt Junior High was in between my house and St. Anthony's School, where I went to school from kindergarten to fourth grade.

One day in fourth grade, there was a rumor that spread around the school about a brawl between Roosevelt Junior High and St. Anthony's, which was a kindergarten to 12th grade catholic school. I remember the school dismissing us early and my teacher told us to go right home. My sister, brother, and I walked pretty quickly straight home that day. I was scared. Although I didn't know anyone at Roosevelt at the time, what I did know was that they were students of color. I never heard if there was a brawl or fight that day. This experience wasn't talked about the next day at school and I never processed what really happened. I was left with a warped idea that people of color were violent.

Moving into a diverse community

The near west side of Syracuse was a very diverse community filled with Blacks, Hispanic, and Native Americans. This community at one time was considered one of the poorest urban communities in Syracuse, top ten nationwide. It was very common for different festivals and gatherings to take place in Skiddy Park throughout the year. The schools at this time were still neighborhood schools and many small businesses and churches were still in business. There was a feeling of pride and community in our neighborhood.

The basketball

At Skiddy Park, I was playing basketball one day when I told the guys I needed to go home for dinner. An older Black teen, named Tommy, told me I couldn't have my ball. Tommy said, "OK. Go home, but I am keeping the ball." Tommy was the strongest and biggest Black guy in the neighborhood.

There were a few times I saw Tommy bully and hit others in the park. Some boys were scared and stood down when Tommy entered the park. I went home hurt and upset and told my dad. My dad went over and got the ball back from Tommy. I was a bit nervous for several months every time Tommy came into the park, but eventually, we played basketball together. There was always something between us, the relationship never changed. I believe this experience subconsciously impacted my understanding of race.

One team, one brotherhood

My race narrative identified that not all of my experiences with people of color were negative. There were many positive experiences and relationships with people of color when I was young which helped me form and develop some ideas of antiracism.

In my neighborhood, the park was a central location for all sports. When I walked across the street to the Skiddy Park basketball court or soccer/football on the field, all the boys from the neighborhood played together. That was where I built most of my relationships.

There were guys from Black, Latino, and Native American cultures that came together to play basketball, football, and baseball. During the summer, the guys would get together to play soccer in the park. My friends and I would come together to play against boys in other parks during the summers as I built relationships with the guys of different backgrounds. We played together for one common goal: to represent the neighborhood.

Playing on various teams helped me to see everyone as a family. I was part of a brotherhood when I went to the park. Why couldn't society be like this brotherhood, one where each person brought their talents and skills together for a common goal? The goal of the human family.

Fowler track and field

I got cut from the varsity basketball team in 11th grade and I joined the track team. In my senior year, the track team was very successful. Being young, and honestly, a white male, I was not aware at the time of all the issues with race that were happening around me. I was naive and chose not to see it. Years later, I started to understand how prevalent racism was and how unaware I was of the racism my teammates experienced daily.

Looking back at my track experience, I saw how our predominantly Black and Brown team, with a Black head coach, was treated differently from the other mainly white schools in our area. The biggest incident that started to open my eyes to racism was at the New York State qualifier meet.

We had the fastest time in the mile relay for the section that season coming into the state qualifier meet. The race started with the first two legs of the relay team gaining a 10-meter lead for me. I was running the third leg of the relay. As I headed to the final turn of the 400 meters, I accidently hit the baton off the inside of my right thigh, and it went flying inside the track. Thankfully, I got off and back on the track without hindering anyone. I finished my leg of the relay and passed the baton to the anchor leg. The anchor leg caught everyone and won easily by 15 meters. The league officials and coaches from the other non-city schools tried to disqualify us in the relay from what we could only assume was to prevent us from going to the New York State track meet. I was crushed to hear that we might be disqualified. My three teammates, all amazing young Black men, worked so hard for over two years to get to the state meet, and I put their dreams in jeopardy.

The officials and coaches talked for what seemed like forever about disqualifying us. The first argument was dropping the baton, but it turned out that I could get off the track to the inside and get back on legally as long as I didn't interfere with any other runners. It was legal. The other argument was that the anchor leg had supposedly impeded another runner when he got the baton. Both arguments were false, so why the big fuss? Was it because we beat all of the big-name teams, or was it because of my Black coach and predominantly Black team? Should only teams from the rich, privileged, white schools travel to the State meet? Fortunately, we were not disqualified and moved on.

Once at the New York State meet, my coach had to deal with racism again. We walked around the track at Colgate University the evening before the state meet and another coach approached him. It appeared that they knew each other. The other, a white coach, said, "What's up with the white guy on your team?" My coach responded, in jest, "The section three rule is every relay team has to have a token white." It seemed like an odd response at the time. I have learned since that many Black and Brown people deal with similar racist microaggressions daily.

A woman of grace

After leaving high school, through my college years, and when I was struggling with addiction there were no impactful experiences in my race narrative. When I was hired by the Syracuse City School District to teach and coach, I learned more about how race impacted not only myself, but the community in which I worked and lived. I had the opportunity of working with an amazing, smart, spiritual Black woman, Shirley, who became my mentor and trusted friend. No matter what happened during the years we worked together in the gym, she was there to teach, inspire, and love. Like the kids would say, I was "schooled" every day as I watched her teach students at Levy Middle School. She created a family environment for all students in the gym. Despite circumstances set forth by school policy and procedures, her dealing with the students was free from the racism in our school. She showed me how to love all students with grace. She didn't send disrespectful students to the main office, her response to these kids was much needed love. She knew that society wasn't fair and she wanted her students to know the importance of respect, love, and hard work.

Our gym was a safe haven for the staff and students of color. They knew they would be accepted and loved. The environment was a family, with a strong maternal influence, that loved everyone and would not tolerate disrespect. Where college lacked in teaching me about working in an urban setting, I learned from her.

When I started teaching, I was full of a desire to save the world. I felt that the students should listen and obey me because I was the teacher. I have the degree, the knowledge, and I wanted to help them. As a mentor, Shirley taught me how to:

- Defuse power struggles
- Invest in students
- Identify students who needed special attention
- Treat students fairly
- Teach with compassion
- Understand equity

This was another step of my journey to teach from the heart, not power and control.

The Levy family

One of the biggest lessons I have learned and which I will always treasure was the importance of creating and belonging to a family. Shirley was the one that created a family environment where we all felt welcomed. The family was a no judgment zone; everyone was invited, but not all accepted the invitation. The family always accepted the marginalized and oppressed. The family was a safe place to share and belong because you were a person of value, loved, and never judged based on position or background. There would be picnics at the end of the year, Black History Month celebrations, and amazing potluck lunches. This family helped me get through my separation and divorce. Even after Levy closed, the family would get together to celebrate success and offer comfort when tragedies happened.

One year should have been labeled the year of the practical joker. If you were in the family, you could be a target. Your school yearbook picture from years back would be displayed on the bulletin board. You could find fish on your desk or a present on the hood of your car. The best day was professional development day at the end of the school year. We were supposed to be working on reports and preparing our plans for next year. The next thing I knew, there were upwards of 12 staff running around with super soaker water guns. The hallways were a mess as staff slipped and wiped out. The laughter and joy was unforgettable. Since that experience, I have strived to create a family environment in my teaching, coaching, and Building Men.

I'm biased, really?

One day in the fall, I was going home from soccer practice at Barry Park feeling pretty good about my relationships with my students. This happened before I did any internal work on race and gender, oblivious to my internal condition. I drove down Westcott Street listening to music at the end of a normal day of teaching and coaching. Westcott Street was considered part of the Syracuse University off-campus housing community, known for arts and music. The community not only housed students, but college professors and staff with families in an eclectic environment. Once you crossed over East Genesee Street the neighbor changed to a community that struggled with poverty.

Driving two blocks past Genesee street, I approached the corner of Westcott and East Fayette, there was a group of four boys dressed in jeans, sneakers, and hoodies on the opposite corner just hanging out. The immediate thought I had was these Black boys standing on the corner must be thugs, up to no good. The thought came that fast. You could say automatically. Despite the number of years I worked and lived with people of color, the thought was present. I had these boys labeled as guys that were dealing drugs, using guns, and selling dope on the street corner.

As I pulled up to the stop sign, one of the boys noticed my car and yelled at me, "Hey Horan." I looked over and there were four young Black men I have known for five years and who were members of the Building Men Program. I rolled down my window and all four boys came up to my car. We shook hands and had a short conversation, checking up on their grades and activities. They asked me about Levy Middle School and Building Men. We talked until the stopped traffic behind me started to honk.

These boys were in the Building Men Program for two years and they were my boys who I have spent years teaching, coaching, and loving. We spent endless hours in school and out of school together. The racist bias in my mind had judged them unfairly. I loved them just as I loved my own son, but that bias still came into my mind. How was I conditioned to fear and judge the boys I love just because of the color of their skin? It was like getting hit with a two-by-four upside my head. This internal work on racism was not optional. I must take an in-depth look at racism. Otherwise, how could I effectively teach, coach, and mentor?

Worst chalk talk ever

In the winter of 2016, during the 10th year of the Building Men Program, I assumed I had a good handle on my biases. After the work I did in the MOST club and 12 Men Model I was feeling pretty confident I was on the right path forward. I had no idea how deep racism resided in me. I was asked to speak to the boys in the Building Men Program at Danforth Middle School. I didn't realize the unfinished internal work concerning Danforth School. I showed up with my pride and well thought Chalk Talk, not a great combination.

A Chalk Talk is a PowerPoint consisting of quotes and videos on a topic to teach the boys about character. This is a time of discussion on character traits we want our boys to obtain. We use a playbook to record definitions, answer questions, and participate in activities to further investigate the character. We are intentional about teaching character, not just hoping it will show up in the program.

Being the director of the Building Men Program, I was going to inspire these youth. I started the character presentation for a dozen or so Black and Brown sixth and seventh grade boys in the program. I learned more about myself and Building Men during this 45 minute session than they did.

The Chalk Talk didn't go smoothly. I stood up with my arrogance expecting everyone to listen to me. I was the boss. I introduced myself and the topic of the Chalk Talk, then the unthinkable happened. Over the course of the next 10 minutes, three boys came in late and started catching up on what happened over the weekend like I wasn't even in the room. One boy showed me his phone. His mom was calling, and he took the call and started talking. By the way, when in a school setting, every time a middle school student has a phone call during the school day, it is their mom. Out of the blue, another student opened the door to yell something in the classroom to his friend. A boy in the back of the room never looked up from his phone. Two boys in the back corner of the room held their own private conversation. I asked them to pay attention and they ignored me completely. I couldn't believe that boys were not paying attention. I wasn't going to let them distract me from helping them, and I plowed through the presentation. The staff removed one boy, and another needed to leave early. I tried my best to keep my composure and be calm as I completed the session. I thanked the staff for letting me speak with the boys and left with an uneasy feeling in my heart.

After processing, I found many lessons within the 45 minute Building Men Chalk Talk experience. I asked myself these few questions to help process my feelings. Who do I think I am that a group of inner-city sixth and seventh grade boys should listen to? Why do I believe my title should earn their respect? Why was I uneasy at Danforth? What prevented me from making a connection?

Here was what I learned. The boys needed to know me before they could connect. I had no relationship with them. My title doesn't earn their trust. I must share with them who I really am, the times I was hurt and failed, the times I felt alone and unworthy of love. I didn't let them relate to my struggles; therefore I didn't connect with them on a human level. This is what earns their respect. I needed to be the guy that would deposit love over time and be able to be there before I could earn the privilege to stand in front of these boys and tell them about character and success. I needed to let them know I would be there for them over the long haul.

After I reflected, I came to the conclusion that I wouldn't listen to me either.

Jerry

One of the boys I met that day was Jerry. When I asked this sixth grader his name he told me a fake name, Jerry. He was a typical sixth-grade boy who didn't want to listen to a guest speaker. All he wanted to do was get into the gym to play basketball. Over the next three years, I would regularly visit the Danforth Building Men Program. Jerry joined its after-school program, and he joined the Building Men Summer Institute. Every time I saw Jerry, I would stop and say, "Hi Jerry." The staff and students would look at me funny when I called him Jerry, everyone else knew that wasn't his name. Over the next three years, we developed a mutual respect and a fondness for each other as our conversations continued to grow in length and he continued in the program. He saw that I was there over the long haul. These boys needed consistency and stability in their lives. He recognized that I cared, and our relationship grew. To me he will always be Jerry.

Dig deeper

By working through my narrative on race, I realized the experience of fear from my younger days impacted me as I presented the Chalk Talk for the boys at Danforth School. Danforth Middle School was the new name for Roosevelt Junior High. Subconsciously, I was afraid, even as an adult, because I never processed the feelings I experienced when I was in fourth grade. Every time I walked into Danforth, I brought my fourth-grade self with me. This fear, racism, and negative energy influenced my ability to help, support, and love the boys with my whole heart. This was a bias I needed to be honest about and seek forgiveness and healing. By honestly facing the bias and seeing the situation for what it really was, I was able to open my heart.

After completing the race narrative, I understand the need to honestly learn, reflect, and search my attitudes and actions of racism. It is my responsibility to do the internal work. My journey with racism and becoming an anti-racist was vital to my growth as a man.

My Lessons

The journey of unpacking the construct of race in my life needed to be intentional. Racism has influenced my decision making, biases, and relationships with adults and my students. Here are the lessons from my past experiences that influence my view on race.

- The experiences of race influenced how I perceived and related to students
- Being unaware of biases helped me justify poor treatment of students and athletes
- Understanding the race narrative in my life helps and heals my heart
- Everyone needs to do the internal work dealing with race to teach, coach, and mentor students
- Everyone is responsible for their education and knowledge of racism
- I need to check my unconscious bias daily
- I need to connect with all students through love and empathy to make the difference

Your Turn:

- How has race impacted your formative years in school? Has race influenced your view as a teacher, coach, or youth worker?
- Have you reflected on the impact race has on your life?
- Who can help you gain a better understanding of different races?

CHAPTER 9

Building Men

As I MENTIONED before, I found a purpose and passion within my heart as I founded Building Men. This journey of creating the Building Men Program fostered growth, healing, and opportunities for personal development. It's led me to many new questions to answer, connected me with men with greater wisdom, and experiences to teach me and others how to be "A" man and not "the" man.

The following experiences were instrumental in the creation and implementation of Building Men, which not only transformed my heart but led to the transformation of the hearts of others.

Vincent House after-school program

When I look back at my life when I was growing up, I was blessed with some answers to questions that were not even asked yet. The basic framework of Building Men was a part of my experience from the very beginning. It was as if I was being prepared to do a job without knowing the job existed. Like I have heard many times, your gifts will make room for you. Some of the core concepts of Building Men first showed up through my childhood experiences at Vincent House. I attended the after-school program at the Vincent House on the west side of Syracuse in my middle school years. At Vincent House, college students served as mentors a few days a week. We would hang out, play games, and talk about guy things. Additionally, participants went on college visits, camped in the summer, and took field trips. A highlight of my experience with Vincent House was going to Buffalo for a basketball tournament.

Vincent House was part of the Catholic Charities Youth Basketball League at the time. We played other community centers around Syracuse. One weekend, we went to a tournament in Buffalo, New York. The trip was so much fun as we traveled in the van for three hours, played two games, went out to eat, and returned home. I don't remember the score. I think we earned a split: won one, lost one. The one part I will never forget was the camaraderie among my teammates. The trip was great, the best part of the experience was the relationships and time spent with my teammates. I would remain friends with these guys throughout high school. It felt like I belonged to something bigger than myself, a brotherhood or fellowship. I fit in somewhere. It wasn't just based on my basketball skills, because I was average at best. The sense of belonging came from living in the same neighborhood. Experiencing life in the inner-city, our community, was what we had in common. These relationships helped me navigate middle school and high school. This band of brothers gave me a group in which to feel a part and belong. This became the basis for the Building Men Program.

Building Men beginnings

Before Building Men there was an after-school intramural basketball program that was developed by two social studies teachers and the principal before I began working at Levy Middle School in 1993. To participate in the intramural basketball program, the boys needed to have their teachers complete a weekly academic and behavior progress report for them. The better they did, the more points their team would receive. The team that won each game received victory points. Victory points and academic points were added together to create the league standings for all the teams. The champion was determined by total points, victory points, and academic progress points. Typically, the team with the best academic and behavioral performance won the championship. A great life lesson by the way. This helped motivate the young men to work harder in their classes and have good attendance and behave better in school. We wanted to help create success habits for their future.

When I started working at Levy Middle School, as a volunteer coach, I won two championships. As a teacher assistant at the time, I would spend time hunting down my players making sure they did all their work and didn't get put into in-school suspension. We were supposed to have a study hall before the game, my study hall was more like a halftime chalk talk. We would go over my plays. I treated it as a professional basketball league. I was overly competitive for an intramural basketball league; I think I might have been the only staff to get a technical foul. When the main social studies teacher, who was the coordinator of the intramural program, transferred to a different school, I took over as the program coordinator.

Belonging to the brotherhood

I began to look at what changes in the intramural after-school program I could make to teach the boys character values. From my experience, I knew I needed to keep the boys physically active and create a brotherhood in which they could push each other towards greatness. Through researching ways of teaching character, positive life principles, and values through the shared experiences. My goal was to develop an after-school program that could challenge the young boys' thinking around societal norms. This concept of developing a brotherhood, a character-based program, and a new way of approaching manhood was called the Building Men Program.

I started slowly over time, through trial and error, adding different aspects to the intramural program and creating Building Men. Through my journey within, I realized one of the important aspects of the program was a sense of belonging. It didn't matter who you were and how well you played, you belonged. We stressed belonging; everyone was of value. As the program developed, we created roles for guys that didn't play sports, as we all were on the journey towards manhood. I knew from my own life that these young boys in middle school needed a place to belong, a brotherhood, and the opportunity to work together towards a common goal.

Put your own mask

As a result of reading *The Season of Life* and attending the InsideOut training, the thought occurred to me, why couldn't I try some of the same activities in the Building Men program that Joe Ehrmann did with his football team? I needed to find a way to touch the hearts of the boys. One big lesson I learned at the training was I needed to be "right" inside my heart to help others. Like they tell you on an airplane, put your own mask on first.

This internal work consisted of self-reflection, healing, reconciliation, and talking with other men about these emotions about winning, losing, and real competition. By developing these authentic relationships with men for the first time in my life, I experienced a closeness and love I never knew before. Instead of spending time discussing sports, teaching or coaching, our conversations opened a world of emotions and feelings I never knew existed. I avoided talking about emotions for most of my life, thinking a strong man doesn't talk about feelings – that it's wimpy. These men helped me put labels on emotions that I'd had all my life. These men knew the real me, accepted me in my brokenness and wanted to spend time with me in a relationship. My friendships and relationships become more real and rich.

Be "A" man, not "the" man

This was my journey to manhood, or as my friend Don would say, "how to be 'A' man not 'the' man." From the moment he made that statement, it has become the Building Men motto. Don was a man I had a hard time figuring out. I was drawn to him when we first started teaching together. In the beginning, I thought he was a good teacher, ball player, and all-around funny guy. Over the course of years watching him teach, I noticed that his empathy and compassion for others was the true reason others were drawn to him. His classroom was a safe place, a space the students could act like themselves without being disrespected or condemned. Kids loved hanging out with him, and he spoke from his heart. Sure, he is one of the funniest guys I know, but it's the love that helps him stand apart from others.

The real Coach Carter

The concept of placing academic success over athletic playing time, looked like it was taken right out of the movie *Coach Carter.* One of our favorite guest speakers was the "real" Coach Carter. Although much shorter in person than Samuel L. Jackson, his message and love for the boys was nothing short of amazing! The way he strived to help improve his boys' academics and the value they had for education was real. Coach Carter reinforced to the boys the knowledge that education helps level the playing field for our youth. I made it a goal every year to teach each young man to be accountable for their education and work to continually motivate them to make academics a priority.

To help the boys look toward future goals we brought in guest speakers to discuss the importance of education in their own journeys. No matter how fun and exciting the activities we offer were, the boys' favorite part of Building Men was when men from the community share their personal experiences. The stories told by men from their own community who rose to success as "A" man show them that success was possible. Men from all different backgrounds explained to the young men about how being successful in life started by being successful in school. Our middle school boys relate to the guest speakers from their neighborhood who look like them and were credible messengers. Many heart connections were made during the question and answer sessions after our guest speakers.

Post-game conference

It was easy to recognize the overly competitive traits in many middle school boys because I had been that boy. My self-worth was connected to winning most of my life. I lost some great relationships with people due to my need to win. I didn't want these amazing boys to grow up and believe that the outcome of the game determines their manhood or worth.

When Building Men started, we had a hard time discovering the way to teach this concept of sportsmanship after a hard fought basketball game. The competition was heated, which was not bad, but after the game, the locker room was hotter. How could we teach healthy competition while maintaining relationships? We wanted the boys to become a part of a larger brotherhood and support each other in and out of the gym, not be at each other's throats after a game.

During one season, we had a volunteer coach, RJ, that didn't know very much about basketball but was a guru on debriefing activities and life skills. He was our school counselor and he loved the adventure experiential education concept. Learning by doing and talking about what we learned from the experience was his jam. Unfortunately, after each game during this particular season, I needed to be in the locker room to ensure no fights broke out and trash talking stopped at the end of the games. After one game, I remember RJ said, "Why don't we debrief the game?" The initial thought inside my head was, "No, I don't want to talk about feelings." The more RJ and I spoke, the more the idea of debriefing made sense. How did I expect the boys to learn how to deal with winning and losing properly if we didn't teach them? In my life, I couldn't manage my feelings until I could identify and talk about each emotion. Even in college basketball, after the game, there was a cooling off period to get in touch with their emotions before the press can interview the players.

I asked for RJ's help to lead the debriefing of the games. We held, what we called, post-game conferences after each game in the weight room. This was the start of developing a culture of brotherhood and healthy competition. At the end of the game, in most youth sports, the boys would walk in a line and shake hands with the opponents and say, "good game." Most times, what you would see was the boys on the losing team walking with their heads down giving half-hearted congratulations, if the players said anything at all. Now after a Building Men game, the boys on both teams take a minute to cool off, sit in a circle, and discuss what had happened. This helped the players process the game and the emotions that came along with winning or losing. We covered many aspects of the game including teamwork, character, and manhood. Through this process, we discussed how an individual doesn't gain or lose value because of the end result/score of the game. We shared how to improve and work together toward a common goal. At the end of the day, we are all young men in the same school, same program, on the same journey to manhood. We would end the post-game conference by handing out sportsmanship coins, our Building Men creed, and the Let's Go cheer. This time debriefing the games together helped calm emotions, gain perspective, and restore value and self-worth to our young men.

The boys don't buy into Building Men because we have cool activities, great academics, or food, they show up because there is a safe space for hearts that seeks love, care, and respect.

Faith — the game changer

After the championship game during the second year, all the boys had left the locker room on their way home. I was closing shop and watching ESPN. As I hung out in my office, two of our volunteer coaches, Mike and Don, came in to say good night.

I was struggling with a hard decision concerning our field trip. We had planned the first rite of passage trip and ceremony for the eighth graders. Building Men had no funding to pay for staff or extra programming. The district provided the gym and equipment, for which we remain forever grateful. We were responsible for everything else. We felt strongly about taking these eighth graders on a rite of passage culminating trip. We were hoping to provide an experience to embed the lessons learned in Building Men which could transform their hearts and minds as they prepare for high school.

The Rite of Passage trip and ceremony was developed to create a significant landmark in the journey towards manhood. We want to prepare the young men for the transition from middle school to high school. We created a day with challenges, discussions, and reflection to help middle school boys transition to the next level with knowledge, confidence, and courage. Years later, many boys remember the lessons and emotions of the Rite of Passage trip, and even still cherish the item of significance which was given to them.

We lacked the funds for the rite of passage trip and I didn't know where the remaining money would come from. I said to Mike and Don, "Hey what should I do? I don't have enough money for all the expenses for the trip. Do I write the check or cancel the trip?" Almost in unison, Mike and Don said: "Write the check." So in their presence, I took the step of faith and filled out the check for Orenda Springs Experiential Education Center and went to Wegmans to order the food.

I have come to understand that Building Men was created for a greater purpose, and as a result, we have been involved in many divine occurrences. Over the years, many things have happened that I can't explain. Things of faith and grace. The next day, my wife called me while I was at work. She told me that we received a check in the mail for the exact amount I spent for the Rite of Passage trip – from someone who wanted to give to the program. I began to feel a sense of power driving this program and providing for our young men. This program became more than a group of guys playing basketball after school. A new journey had begun, one that I never expected or anticipated, a purpose to impact others.

Cross Training Athletics

Occasionally, I would check Joe Ehrmann's website to see if he was speaking near Syracuse. I found out he was scheduled to speak at a conference in Buffalo, NY. I thought this would be a great opportunity to connect with Joe and learn more. Signing up to attend the conference, I didn't know at the time that I had a divine appointment to meet another man that would impact Building Men.

I met the founder of Cross Training Athletics and the author of the creed, Coach Mike Masters, who was presenting at the same conference. His presentation was on teaching leadership and character through sports, I was intrigued with his Cross Training Athletics program. His program was growing throughout high school and college sports teams in western New York. His goals were very similar to what we were doing in Building Men.

At one of the breaks, I introduced myself and asked if we could get a cup of coffee and talk about his program. A few weeks later I drove a couple of hours to the Buffalo, NY area to meet him. I figured I would be there for an hour and get back to school in time to do a few things before the end of the day. Three and a half hours later, I left his office to return to Syracuse. I was completely blown away by his amazing work of bringing character into sports and schools. He developed a character theme for the sports' season and playbook for coaches to use with their teams. For example, one theme was Finish Strong. Each letter stood for a character trait: faith, integrity, never quit, etc. I learned more about rewarding and emphasizing character. He used movie clips, videos, as well as quotes to drive home his points. He had a great way to use ordinary objects to teach lessons on character, which helps our boys relate and conceptualize each character trait.

We established a partnership, and Building Men started using his character-based programs. I enjoyed using the object lessons to teach character. I could imagine having a toolbox filled with objects to teach character skills. The most important message I received from Coach was that love never fails. Coach Masters let us use his creed as the Building Men Creed.

Our Creed
Build the Heart of a Champion from the Inside out.
I will Believe, Think, Love, and Work with ALL MY Heart
I will fear no one, I will respect everyone
There is no such thing as staying the same
Yesterday is over and can't be changed
So I'll give 100% today
To be the most Complete Player I can be,
Physically, Mentally, Socially, and in Spirit.
My Motto is simple: Know what's right, Do what's right.
Win with Humility and Lose with Grace.
I will fight the good Fight
I will finish the race
I will keep the Faith
*Used with Permission from Cross Training Athletics

Circle process

One day, a colleague told me about an upcoming training on restorative circles that sounded intriguing. She said this would be great for Building Men and encouraged me to attend. I received permission to attend the training from my principal and registered for the training right away. The first day of the training session was inspiring. I learned about using circles to discuss, restore, and heal relationships. This was the strategy and technique Building Men needed to provide a safe space to help young men process an experience, discuss emotions, ask questions about manhood, and grow into self-aware young men.

What I didn't expect to happen during the training was a stirring in my heart. Midway through the training, I felt a strong desire in my heart to be back in middle school. At that time, I was teaching kindergarten to fifth grade physical education at Hughes Elementary school. I had a very comfortable, light teaching schedule, which I felt I deserved and had earned. This desire to return to middle school was a strong internal feeling, the type I normally would push down and try to ignore. This feeling wouldn't stay silent. There was a longing to be at the middle school level working with the boys daily. I left the training and spoke with my wife and mentors. By the end of the next week I talked to my principal about moving to H.W. Smith Pre-K to 8. I felt at peace after that conversation knowing that I was on my way to H.W. Smith, not only to teach but to start another Building Men Program. What I did not know at the time was this decision would bring Building Men to the next level.

Building Men in the classroom

Shortly after I moved to H.W. Smith, the principle called me into her office for a conversation. She was explaining to me that H.W. Smith was an extended time learning school, which means the day is longer and the students have an enrichment class. She introduced me to the staff at Peaceful School who were in charge of teaching the enrichment classes. Then the principal said, "OK, Joe is going to teach a Building Men class." I was taken a bit off guard, I said, "OK." She went on to explain that instead of teaching physical education every period, "You are going to teach one enrichment class of Building Men." I was excited and nervous all at the same time. I had an opportunity to teach manhood to a class of seventh graders during the school day. Let the adventure begin.

In the Building Men class, I experimented with ways of engaging young boys in learning about character. Some techniques that we found were successful in engaging boys in the after-school program worked within the classroom as well. The daily exposure and interaction with character in the class started to change the climate of the school. Some different methods that worked consisted of motivational and character videos, book clubs, project-based learning, academic progress monitoring, and incentive days. Most important method was touching the heart of the students.

The positive classroom experience set the stage for our Building Men elective classes throughout the district. The key component was to have teachers and students work together to make education relevant to their future. All the while creating a brotherhood of young men working together for success. As the school embraced Building Men strategies, there became a change in the school climate. This sparked a change in the mindset of the students. Not only had this impacted the mindset of the boys, but also affected the hearts of the teachers. Many teachers shared they gained a new energy and sense of inspiration from Building Men.

Learning from the boys

Nashon and Chaz were members of Building Men in middle school. When they attended Nottingham High School they taught me about unity and brotherhood. We had a tradition of doing community service during our mid-winter break. On the Tuesday of break, we made bag lunches for a men's homeless shelter. As Building Men grew we had two days of community service to get more boys involved, one at Levy Middle School on the east side of the city and the other at Clary Middle School in the southernmost part of the city. We had a great time Tuesday at Levy, making over

50 bag lunches for the homeless, eating some pizza, and playing basketball with about 25 boys. Clary was scheduled to have its event the following day.

Tuesday around 3:00 pm after the community service event, I received a call from Chaz saying he was sorry for missing making sandwiches. I told him if he really wanted to participate, he still could by attending the community service event at Clary the next day. I didn't think that it would happen, as he didn't know any of the Clary staff or middle school boys from the south side of town.

To my surprise, Nashon and Chaz attended the community service event at Clary Middle School. I was told by the Clary staff that not only did they attend, but they led the Clary boys by showing them how to run the sandwich making assembly line. Nashon and Chaz taught me that Building Men was not about being involved in one particular school, it was about belonging to the Building Men brotherhood! Building Men provided a belonging and unity for boys in the city.

The logo lesson

This was one of those out of the blue, unexpected lessons I learned from the young men. The theme of this lesson was I should never stop checking my predetermined judgments. It happened when we sought to create a peer mentoring program in high school. We took 20 high school boys to a Leadership Conference in Liverpool, run by Team Adventure, to encourage and inspire them to be leaders at Nottingham High School. Team Adventure was an organization that runs team building sessions to help people develop teamwork and leadership skills. We wanted to instill leadership skills into these boys so they could mentor others.

There was a young man named Tyquan, an eleventh grader who attended the field trip. I taught Tyquan in middle school. We never really clicked in physical education class or Building Men. My relationship was neutral, I can't say it was good or bad. At that time in my career, I was struggling with valuing all students with the same love and understanding.

If I didn't have a good relationship with you, I didn't give you the same love and value as others. I realized that I was not a good teacher to all children earlier in my teaching career.

As the facilitators were giving the presentation on how to improve the Building Men Program, Tyquan was doodling during the session. In the typical off-topic Tyquan way, he said, "Here is a new logo we should use." I loved it. Here is one of the boys that I didn't click with, showed problematic behaviors in middle school, and what does he do? He created a sketch that would become our official logo.

Tyquan created a logo that looked like the Arm & Hammer baking soda logo, a strong arm with a hand holding a hammer. Tyquan drew it freehand. It read: "We have the power." I brought the logo to my principal. He liked it but wanted to change the hammer into a diploma, because there is power in education. I couldn't argue with that. Once again, I learned the lesson from my students, my biases can get in the way of loving and teaching all students. I will always remember Tyquan and the logo.

Let's go

After each Building Men session, we close by repeating the creed, followed by saying "Let's go." The signature way to say "let's go" was developed by Coach Lefler. Coach Lefler was a longtime PE teacher and coach at Clary Middle School. In 2007, Coach Lefler started Building Men at Clary Middle School. It is currently the longest, continuous-running program in the Syracuse City School District (16 years at the writing of this book). I haven't done much in the program without him. He was one of the legends of the program, as his love for the young men was unparalleled.

The original and official "Let's go" cheer goes like this: Visualize standing in a circle of young middle school men, take a good athletic position with a slight bend at the knees, one leg out in front the other, with one arm extended out in front of you. Using the extended arm, loosen the wrist, put your first finger and middle finger together, and on the count of three you shake your wrist and say, "Let's go". The leader of the day, either staff or young men, counted "one, two, three," followed by three claps and a loud and enthusiastic "Let's go." This has become the traditional way of ending each session. The "Let's go" cheer has morphed into many variations. The longer you are in the program, the more variations you will learn.

Personally, I don't see "Let's go" as an ending. It's a new beginning. This was not only a way to bring the boys together at the end of the session, but a reminder that we are all in one program and on one journey towards manhood. It has been my prayer that we were sending our young men forth on a positive trajectory, into our communities as "A" man. "A" man that will be a positive light in the lives of friends, family, and the community.

One, two, three, Let's go!

My Lessons

The journey of founding Building Men has helped me continue to do the internal work and learn how to lead and teach from my heart. The challenge of finding ways to engage the boys in conversations and activities to help them get in touch with their authentic selves was my internal drive. Here are the lessons that influenced the creation of Building Men.

- The boys want to belong to a brotherhood
- Young men need a safe space to learn how to share our emotions and hurts
- The value of education is vital to success
- Connect their education with their purpose and passion
- Teaching character through sports, quotes, videos, and object lessons helps the boys gain a better understanding
- Living in this society that stresses success and achievement, there is a need to learn how to deal with failure and mistakes from a mental health standpoint
- My judgments/biases cloud my ability to teach, accept and help others

- The process of self-assessment needs to be continual

Your Turn:

- How have your interactions with students impacted your views as a teacher, coach or youth worker?
- Are there personal biases or judgments that prevent you from helping all students?
- What passion do you have that you can use to connect with your students?
- How can you make learning exciting and relevant?

The Journey never ends

WHEN I FELT the need to help the middle school boys avoid the pain I experienced, I had no idea where the Building Men journey would take me. Learning from the experiences of my past, searching for the truth within, and opening my heart to mentors led me deep into my heart. This journey inspired and motivated me to teach others how to become "A" man, finding their purpose and truth. Building Men was a way to connect with the hearts of students so they can find their authentic selves.

When I humbled myself to look for the greater story in my life, the lessons, the experiences good and bad, as well as the people who inspired and taught me, it came together like a jigsaw puzzle called Building Men. My understanding of being "A" man, not "the" man was a culmination of my life experiences. This would not have been possible without the people that were divinely placed in my life. My desire was to help young men by providing wisdom and direction to walk their own journey to manhood. Doing my inside work, answering the hard questions, and reflecting on how others have impacted my life started the creation of a program that will provide positive experiences and a loving environment to help others grow.

Learning from life's lessons

The lessons which I experienced and learned over the course of my life created something good, something positive was birthed through my pain. These were some of the larger life lessons that impacted my journey in the Building Men Program.

The group-mentoring environment was a result of the local community center, camps, teen seminar, and sports teams that I belonged to during my younger years. By having a place in which I belonged and was accepted, I stayed in school. Although I didn't always make great decisions and took a few detours, my true north brought me back where I needed to be.

In Building Men, we strived to create a safe space to talk and belong. Everything I did was designed to bring boys together and provide a feeling of belonging and worth. I have watched, learned, and studied how different teachers in various subject areas and coaches in different levels of sports create a loving and caring environment for their students. They open their hearts and lives to these students to create a safe and nurturing environment. In the safe space, students were able to learn and transformation can happen.

Our curriculum is centered around the concept of being "A" man not "the" man. The definition of "A" man grew into the acronym S.I.R. Someone with Significance, Integrity, and who values and builds Relationships.

- Significance – live for a cause greater than yourself
- Integrity – become complete and whole, trust your heart
- Relationships – Value and build positive relationships with others

These three character traits became the core values of Building Men. As I learned through my own experience, when I began seeking significance rather than selfishness, my life started to turn the corner. When I found my significance, I also found my worth and purpose. I needed to share this part of my journey with the young men who joined Building Men.

As I became honest with myself and followed my True North, I found a way of living filled with peace and no longer needed to perform for others. It was only through starting to live a life of integrity that my purpose and gifts started to surface in my life. Through having honest relationships based on trust and care, I started to win in life. This was the turning point. The positive relationships with the great men that were placed in my life, provided me healing and helped me be able to grow in wisdom and understanding.

Looking at the core values of S.I.R. (significance, integrity, and relationships), I began to take activities and transform them into experiences to touch the hearts of the young men. I turned the mid-winter vacation open gym into an annual community service tradition. This provided an opportunity to discuss the importance of giving back to our community.

The desire and joy the boys found in giving to others was the catalyst in creating the community crew. As I wanted to share with the boys what I learned and experienced with Zac, this led to the desire to take the boys on a mission trip. One group of eighth graders from the second year of Building Men class at H.W. Smith really enjoyed doing monthly community service projects. These young men grew into the community crew and their friendship turned them into a close-knit group. They met monthly for a community service project over the next three years. The years of community service ended in traveling to El Salvador to serve in a developing country. The shared experience built lasting relationships that are still solid today.

I knew I had to teach my boys about integrity. One way I learned how to live a life of integrity was to learn from other men's examples. We invited community role models into Building Men as guest speakers as part of our chalk talks. We sought out men to speak from the heart so we can learn and develop. The guest speakers engaged us in learning together what "A" man was in our community.

The importance of learning from others' experiences led us to create the Leadership Conferences. By partnering with other programs and being blessed with funding, we brought national speakers into a professional conference setting to impact our young men. The conference experience gave the boys exposure to a different way of learning. The conferences had breakout sessions on different aspects of manhood and provided in-depth conversations for personal growth. Our aim was to give the boys an experience and exposure to build a future where they can strive for success.

Summer Institute

In 2012, I started by incorporating Building Men activities into the half-day summer school program. We had a chance to pilot the character talks both in the classroom and in the gym. The pilot project turned into the development of the Building Men Summer Institute. The summer institute was a full day program for middle school boys. Our goal was to provide a full day of the Building Men experience to our boys. The morning consisted of fitness, academics, character, book break, and lunch. We strived to teach boys as boys with project-based learning, games, and some competition. Believing in not only their capability to handle the academic work, but in their greatness to rise to new levels. The afternoon consisted of character talks, manhood sessions, guest speakers, field trips, and athletics. The summer institute grew into a summer school program offered at four middle schools over the next few years.

Rite of passage

As Building Men grew, a larger question presented itself. How do we embed the important conversations about becoming "A" man in our boys' hearts? I wanted the boys to have the courage to hold tight to their personal values and not conform to society. I learned through experience when I didn't hold tight to my personal values, I made poor choices that had a negative impact on my life. We were planting seeds of character and value into the hearts of young men, therefore, we needed the patience for them to grow and develop.

We realized the need for a culminating activity at the end of the program to further nurture the seed. This inspired the creation of the Rite of Passage trip and ceremony. The Rite of Passage started as a field trip to Orenda Springs to complete a ropes course experience and allow boys to reflect on their Building Men experience. Over the next couple years, we added character lessons that were connected to life situations they would face in high school. Currently, the Rite of Passage is an overnight trip experience with 10 different life lessons reinforced through day-long initiatives, reflections, stories, and a fireside ceremony filled with ritual and emotion. The power of this trip has transformed the lives of the young men.

White ribbon campaign

The discussions in the MOST Club about domestic and sexual violence would lead to the boys participate in Vera House's White Ribbon Campaign. Our young men would help by selling the white bracelets to raise awareness of the problems of domestic and sexual violence in our community. As the partnership grew, we started taking boys to the actual White Ribbon Breakfast and participated in the White Ribbon Walk in downtown Syracuse. The young men experienced walking with others in the community, seeing themselves as part of something bigger. We wanted to expand their experience during the walk and brought in a keynote speaker before the walk. We invited men in the community to join us for lunch after the walk to debrief their experience. We found another avenue to show our boys how to grow into men that can impact the community.

High school

As the Building Men grew to different middle schools and the boys moved up to high school, another question by the boys arose: "When would Building Men be offered in high school?" This question hit my heart as I reflected on what helped me all through my high school experience. Building Men needed to become a place where the youg men could feel safe and belong. We wanted to provide a group of friends that would insulate each other from some of the negative pressure high school entails. This led to the development of Building Men in the high schools, a safe space to belong. In the high schools, a Building Men would develop into a leadership group, Men of Strength club, and a career building course over the course of four years.

Building Men continued to grow and develop to help young men in my community. As I continue to seek help and take the inside journey, I am inspired and energized with the purpose I was called to fulfill. This new path to transforming the hearts of young men, led to my transformation and greatest success.

Your journey to success

My journey to success has become one of transformation. In earlier years, I was all about transactional success. The change in my life happened by getting help from others, doing self-reflection, prayer, and transforming deep inside my heart. I welcome you to join me on a transformational journey. It's hard. I am not going to lie. I still cringe when I see more work to be done, but it must be done to set the standard and example for the next generation. I've found when I drop the insecurities, fears, false standards, racism, and implicit biases I can learn unconditional love. Choose to love without judgment. I use this new knowledge to help me grow into the best version of myself.

What is your definition of success in this journey? Is it becoming the best version of you? Having a heart that inspires others? Using your gifts to bless, touch, and transform the hearts of our youth?

It was my hope in writing this book, sharing my pain and life lessons, in the hope that they will spark something within you to help you on your life's journey. I invite you to take *your* journey. It won't look like mine because the journey is all about being the best version of yourself. I can assure you that your heart, in Building Men we say your "True North", will guide you to become the best version of yourself which will enable you to live your best self. Let's Go!

Some of the books that impacted me were:

- *InsideOut Coaching* by Joe Ehrmann,
- *Quiet Strength* by Tony Dungy
- *Touching Spirit Bear* by Ben Mikaelsen
- *Purpose Living Teen* by Coach D, Darrell Andrews
- *3D Coaching* by Jeff Duke
- *The Secret to Success* by Eric Thomas

The movies that touched my heart were

- *Coach Carter*
- *Antwan Fisher*
- *More Than A Game*
- *Facing the Giants*
- *Finding Forrester*
- *The Pursuit of Happyness*

Author Bio

Joe Horan is the Founder and Executive Director of Building Men Program Inc. based in Syracuse, New York. He holds a bachelor's and master's degree from SUNY Cortland and has 30 years of experience as an educator and coach. The Building Men Program, established in 2006, was created as a space for middle school boys to develop their S.I.R. qualities (Significance, Integrity, and Relationships) and learn how to be "A" Man.

Today, the program has grown into a full district initiative in Syracuse and Joe has become an author, speaker, and trainer. The Building Men Program has been featured in the School Administrators Association of New York State's Vanguard magazine. He has received recognition as a teacher/coach by Parents Partnership for Education, Syracuse City School District, NAACP Jr., Coaches of Section III, Vera House Inc., and WSTM Channel 3 for commitment and service to students. He lives in Syracuse with his wife MaryPat and is a father to three amazing children and has two beautiful grandchildren.

Made in United States
North Haven, CT
29 August 2024

56700894R00082